M000101811

Tami Spry

WRITING
PERFOR-
MANCE

To Jessie
For all of the
performances of her
life.
    Your intellect and
heart have enriched
my classroom and my soul.
        Love.
            Tami

Tami Spri

WRITING PERFOR-MANCE

Poeticizing the Researcher's Body

Ronald J. Pelias

Benedictine University Library
Mesa Campus
225 E. Main Street
Mesa, AZ 85201

Southern Illinois University Press
Carbondale and Edwardsville

Copyright © 1999 by the Board of Trustees, Southern Illinois University
All rights reserved
Printed in the United States of America

02 01 00 99   4 3 2 1

Library of Congress Cataloging-in-Publication Data
Pelias, Ronald J.
    Writing performance : poeticizing the researcher's body /
Ronald J. Pelias.
    Includes bibliographical references.

    1. Acting—Psychological aspects. 2. Performing arts. 3. Perfor-
mance art. 4. Theater audiences—Psychology. 5. Body, Human.
I. Title.
PN2058.P46 1999
792'.028'019—dc21   98-37551
ISBN 0-8093-2235-8 (cloth : alk. paper)   CIP

The paper used in this publication meets the minimum requirements of
American National Standard for Information Sciences—Permanence of
Paper for Printed Library Materials, ANSI Z39.48-1984. ⊗

For my teachers,

Joanna H. Maclay
and
Leland H. Roloff

Contents

A Methodological Note

I first remember hearing the phrase "performance is a way of knowing" in graduate school. It was repeated so frequently and with such assurance that its methodological status stood without question or suspicion. We just knew it was true. We knew it in our bodies, from the daily work of performance. We knew it as we talked with one another about our performance experiences. We knew it personally when we discovered that some performances would live with us, like old friends or enemies, inscribing their images and spirits on our psyche. In other words, we knew it as sensuous beings, somatically engaged in performative events. Such knowledge resides in the ontological and is perhaps best expressed in the poetic. This book is about that kind of knowing.

Believing that performance is a way of knowing, I read over the years many production reports, historical essays, and theatre reviews to discover what knowledge the performers had to report. I also attempted to write about my own performance work. These accounts, however, often seemed flat, even boring. They served to document that a particular performance occurred, but in the reporting, they stripped the performance of its life, of its soul. They offered detailed descriptions, objectively presented, often within a theoretical or historical context. They did not capture, however, the performances' artistic pulse. They left out the heart of what attracts us to performance and makes it meaningful. They shared everything except what matters. Perhaps that is too much to expect: No essay can translate the art of the stage to the page.

I basically agree with that last assertion. Yet, I am convinced that to discuss performance without some accounting of its essence as art is, at best, misleading or, more strongly stated, fraud. It is the equivalent of talking about lovemaking without reference to touch. To accept that duplicating the performance experience in essay form may be impossible is not, however, to succumb to silence. A report can establish a metonymic connection to the performance event by privileging the experiential and artistic. When done well, the reader may gain some feel for the event, some understanding of the participants' perspectives, some grasp of its aesthetic power. When well done, the reader senses the dual presence of art, that of the original performance event being discussed and that of the performance event occurring on the page. The artistic or poetic report, then, may possess a kinship, commensurate with, but distinct from, the phenomenon under study.

To strive for such an end locates the performance researcher in an interrelated collection of scholarly assumptions and beliefs. First, to argue that the poetic essay is a powerful way to render a performative experience is to question whether the scientific ideal of objectivity, impartiality, and detachment is an adequate model for writing about performance. Whether knowingly or not, performance scholars have not escaped the considerable institutional authority of positivist logics. Despite years of direct and devastating attacks on positivism, performance scholars, like their cohorts in the other performing arts, humanities, and human sciences, seem incapable of completely dismantling the positivist apparatus. Performance research is still frequently marked by a dispassionate, third person author who proceeds with calculated neutrality as if the descriptive task before him or her is not problematic. But, of course, it is problematic.

It is problematic on two primary counts: (1) analysis is always filtered through a perceiving agent; and (2) analysis can never exhaust its subject. Neither one of these points is new. They typically reside under the familiar postmodern banner "the crisis in representation."[1] The crisis emerges from the increasing skepticism in the modernist belief that we could get it right, that we could nail down, once and for all, the truth. But, as Trinh Minh-ha explains, "One cannot seize without smothering, for the will to freeze (capture) brings about a frozen (emptied) object."[2] "Seizing" and "freezing" are gestures that seek to control and master but ultimately misrepresent and oppress. This follows from the recognition that to represent is to speak as a located self, one who is situated historically and culturally and who is invested in certain discursive and ideological practices that obscure by privileging the present and silencing the absent.

Recognizing the mediating presence and power of the individual and the inexhaustibility of any subject sets in motion a different bias, one that celebrates the multivocal, multilayered, and multivalent realities of everyday life. It insists that all understandings are contingent and contestable. It fears the declarative ("it is"); it lives in the subjunctive ("as if"). It is to be caught, as H. L. Goodall would have it, in the "rock n roll mystery" where

> [t]he communicative dimensions of experience are socially construct*ing* as well as socially construct*ed*. . . . There is, strictly speaking, no one "reality" available to the mutually constructed and constructing communicative dimensions of experience; there are, instead, multiple *copresent* realities.[3]

Pursuing Goodall's "plural present," by modernist standards, is destined to failure: We will never completely capture the diffuse and diverse dynamics of everyday life.

This last point sets up the second underlying assumption to the argument that the poetic essay is a powerful way to render a performative experience. By calling upon the poetic, I discard notions of verification, reliability, and facticity for plural truths rooted in the personal. The poetic essay finds kindred spirits in the diary, the journal, the personal narrative, the confession, the autobiography, not in the objective research report, the factual history, or the statistical proof. The latter, when applied to performance, marks that an event occurred; the former tells of its character. In short, the poetic essay offers a more nuanced account in keeping with the spirit of the performative event itself. The performance scholar, then, might wish to articulate what he/she knows not through the mirroring positivistic logics but through a reliance on the poetic.

I recognize that by calling upon the poetic I do not escape the dangers of representation. As Herbert Blau notes, "The issue in writing is to make it as credible as possible, with intelligence as the measure, before it fails."[4] I understand that to represent is to diminish and that I might choose, with Peggy Phelan or Philip Auslander, to write toward disappearance instead of preservation.[5] I know too, as Janelle Reinelt argues, that to disappear can disable, can render oneself empty, paralyzed.[6] I am reminded of Jill Taft-Kaufman's useful corrective:

> People whose lives form the material for postmodern counter-hegemonic discourse do not share the optimism over the new recognition of their discursive subjectivities, because such an acknowledgment does not address sufficiently their collective historical and current struggles against racism, sexism, homophobia, and economic injustice. They do not appreciate being told they are living in a world in which there are no more real subjects. Ideas have consequences. Emphasizing the discursive self when a person is hungry and homeless represents both a cultural and humane failure.[7]

I turn to the poetic with the hope that I might pursue both the possibilities of disappearance and the power of presence.

Instead of writing a work that hits hard, that is straight to the point, that is based in well-formulated arguments, carefully arranged to leave no room for doubt; instead of crippling my critics, recruiting new members and eliciting new allegiances; instead of being armed, ready for a good fight, ready to enjoy the bounty of conquest, I want to write in another shape. I seek a space that unfolds softly, one that circles around, slides between, swallows whole. I want to live in feelings that are elusive, to live in doubt. I want to offer an open hand that refuses to point but is unwilling to allow injustices to slip through its fingers. I want to be here for the taking, a small figure against the academic wall. I am content to be alone but enjoy the company I keep. I search perpetually for "a momentary stay against confusion."[8]

My desire for the poetic as an alternative mode of representing performance did not emerge in isolation. I enjoy considerable company. In fact, my debts are so large that I can only identify a few of the many contributing voices. First, there are those scholars who wish to preserve the poetic in their research efforts. Elizabeth C. Fine, for example, insists that the aesthetic features of oral performance must be maintained in any adequate translation from the stage to the page. As she says, "The textmaker must decode an aesthetic transaction and recode that transaction in another medium, for another audience, so that they participate vicariously in the original performance."[9] Moving in the opposite direction, from page to stage, Victor Turner, in cooperation with Richard Schechner, turns to performance as a way of breathing life into the standard ethnographic report. Turner maintains that having performances based upon findings from the field is a way of bringing "to human, existential fulfillment what have hitherto been only mentalistic protocols."[10]

Second, there are those scholars who have discovered in the poetic essay an alternative mode of expressing their insights. The New Journalism, for instance, turns objective reporting into novelistic storytelling.[11] Literary critics, perhaps most notably Roland Barthes, show us the "pleasures of the text" in their performative writings. Phenomenologists, such as Gaston Bachelard and Georges Poulet, find in the poetic a way to represent the braiding of the knower and the known. Ethnographers, writing what John Van Maanen calls "impressionist tales," put together an "imaginative rendering of fieldwork" with the intent "to draw an audience into an unfamiliar story world and allow it, as far as possible, to see, hear, and feel as the fieldworker saw, heard, and felt."[12]

Finally, there are those performing artists who weave their personal experiences with theoretical discourse. Craig Gingrich-Philbrook, for example, often places Jacque Lacan's writings against his own experiences as a gay activist in his performance art work.[13] This kind of work, sometimes operating under the banners "performing theory" or "stand up theory," functions to poeticize the theoretical and locate it in the personal. As Elliot Linwood explains:

> Many performance artists are reclaiming the responsibility of the critic by reinserting their own bodies into untested theoretical positions so the public can scrutinize the fit. This bold re-teaching campaign weans theoretical language away from privileged realms by shifting theory's epicenter into the street

somewhere just outside the classroom, slightly offstage. The return of the hypothetical (or applied arts for that matter) now asks whose theory is it anyway?[14]

The turn to the poetic, as Adrienne Rich suggests, is not "a philosophical or psychological blueprint; it's an instrument for embodied experience."[15] As "an instrument of embodied experience," the poetic essay seeks a different standard for presenting the performance event on the page. In other words, if the poetic essay stands as a mode for rendering performance, what might constitute an acceptable and authoritative account? Four criteria suggest themselves: coherence, plausibility, imagination, and empathy.

A coherent poetic essay holds together, gels in an intelligible and articulate manner. Its parts seem to coalesce, to become intertwined, to find relationships with one another. The parts may settle into a seeming unity or may shatter into a disjunctive array. In either case, the parts insist upon some association that yokes them together. As the parts come together in their harmonious and inharmonious combinations, the essay finds its voice, a voice that often cannot be contained within a single speaker.

A plausible poetic essay appears credible. It pulls together a believable combination of the parts. Like a good story, it offers a convincing narrative. It stands as a version, an interpretation among many that appears reasonable to accept. It seeks an internal logic, one that may be filled with ambiguity, tension, and contradictions. Held against the external world, it may echo or challenge everyday understandings. Its account, then, is a temporary diagnosis. It illustrates the possible.

The imaginative poetic essay is literary. It calls upon traditional aesthetic standards, those questioned by literary critics and relied upon by creative writers. It privileges the sensuous, the figurative, the expressive. It calls for an aesthetic transaction, an encounter between the writer and the reader. It demands engagement. Like good phenomenology, it presents through reflection and imaginative free variation the complexity and richness of its subject.

An empathic poetic essay is marked by respect. It strives to feel with others, to understand what others see. It works for a generosity of spirit that creates space for others. It invites dialogue. It is an open invitation for speech, a desire to hear others. The empathic essay, then, privileges an ethics of fairness, sensitive to the ideological consequences of its own discourse and aware that an empathic gesture cannot become a substitute for political action.

Having identified several criteria that characterize a good poetic essay, I might note a few dangers of the form, ones that move beyond the negatives of incoherent, implausible, unimaginative, and nonempathic.

First, writers of the poetic essay risk the appearance of self-indulgence. They may seem unbridled as they attempt to pull personal experience into the scholarly equation. In short, self-consciousness may lead to self-absorption. They may fail to land, as Trinh Minh-ha describes, on the "narrow and slippery ground" between the "twin chasms of navel-gazing and navel-erasing."[16] Second, writers of the poetic essay risk accusations of irrelevance, since they may work without reference to previous scholarly endeavors. In the attempt to achieve the poetic, traditional procedures, such as reviewing the literature, citing sources, and building bibliographies, may be left behind. In such cases, readers may have difficulty placing the work in its scholarly context. Third, writers of poetic essays also risk the charge of irrelevance because they seldom specify how their contributions add to the ongoing knowledge within the field. It is common in the traditional essay for a writer to first identify what has been done on a given topic and then to articulate how his/her essay will explore new terrain. Such markings are typically not done in the poetic essay, since to do so would be an acceptance of the positivist presupposition that knowledge is progressive, always moving toward a goal of obtaining the complete truth. This assumption is one that writers of the poetic essay would reject.

I have intentionally left hanging what I mean by the poetic in the hope that much of what has preceded will inductively enrich the discussion. I am evoking the poetic first to suggest that the essays are something constructed, something made. They are fictions that never assert the truth but strive for the truthful. They are plays that have no final curtain. They seek the ambiguous realities that constitute our performative lives, ambiguities that are often rendered too easily in the more traditional essay. They strive toward the literary with the recognition that the literary is too slippery to define. They are imaginative constructions whose truth lies not in their facticity but in their evocative potentiality. Following Tess Gallagher, I am evoking the poetic as "the point of all possibilities," where time collapses, drawing in the past, present, and future.[17] The poetic is a space of reflection, curving away and back, turning in and out, pulling close and pushing away. It is a place, as Donald Revell describes, of "nextness," where "the next betrays the past, refusing the humble status of aftermath. The next deprivileges the past, voiding its sense of climax."[18]

In short, then, this book is a "writing performance." That is, it is interested in both writing about performance, from the everyday performative routines we enact to the texts we stage, as well as writing performatively, creating texts that vanish as they appear, that live in a complex undecidability, and that reside in the poetic.

Achieving such a goal may be this fool's folly. The essays to follow may be nothing more than feeble attempts. They may fail in meeting the criteria established above. If so, I take some comfort in waiting for other writers whose literary skills are beyond mine to pursue the performative essay as a written mode for presenting performance events.

My efforts to present performance events are organized into three parts: "Performing Every Day," "On Writing and Performing," and "Being a Witness." Part One, "Performing Every Day," focuses upon performances in everyday life, from the daily business of enacting roles to the telling of tales that make life meaningful. Part One incorporates essays about the ongoing process of presenting oneself in everyday life; the gender script that insists that men enact manly performances; the classroom performances of teachers and students; stories of gender, class, and race that mark identity; and a record of the talk I produced in a day's time accompanied with reflections about and responses to that talk. Part Two, "On Writing and Performing," looks at the written script and performance practices. It contains a description of a struggle between a writer and a performer as they protect their own interests; an intimate look at an apprehensive performer; a short play, *The Audition*, about what it means to be an actor; a chronicle of a performance process from the perspective of an actor; and a brief essay on the nature of performance. Part Three, "Being a Witness," examines performance from the perspective of the audience member and the director. It includes essays on the experience of being an audience member; viewing theatre in the context of New York City; directing and being directed by actors' bodies; watching the *DEF Comedy Jam*; and some final reflections about working with performance for many years in the form of an interview.

Notes

1. For rich discussions of this concept, see Jean-François Lyotard, *The Postmodern Condition: A Report on Knowledge*, trans. Geoff Bennington and Brian Massumi (Minneapolis: University of Minnesota Press, 1984); Hal Foster, ed., *The Anti-Aesthetic: Essays on Postmodern Culture* (Port Townsend: Bay Press, 1983).

2. Trinh T. Minh-ha, *Woman, Native, Other: Writing Postcoloniality and Feminism* (Bloomington: Indiana University Press, 1989), 61.

3. H. L. Goodall Jr., *Living in the Rock n Roll Mystery: Reading Context, Self, and Others as Clues* (Carbondale: Southern Illinois University Press, 1991), 213.

4. Bonnie Marranca and Gautam Dasgupta, "The Play of Thought: An Interview with Herbert Blau," *Performing Arts Journal* 14 (September 1992): 27.

5. Peggy Phelan, *Unmarked: The Politics of Performance* (New York: Routledge, 1993); Philip Auslander, *Presence and Resistance: Postmod-*

ernism and Cultural Politics in Contemporary American Performance (Ann Arbor: University of Michigan Press, 1992).

6. Janelle Reinelt, "Staging the Invisible: The Crisis of Visibility in Theatrical Representation," *Text and Performance Quarterly* 14 (April 1994): 97–107.

7. Jill Taft-Kaufman, "Other Ways: Postmodern and Performance Praxis," *Southern Communication Journal* 60 (spring 1995): 226.

8. Robert Frost, "The Figure a Poem Makes," *Robert Frost on Writing*, ed. Elaine Barry (New Brunswick: Rutgers University Press, 1973), 126.

9. Elizabeth C. Fine, *The Folklore Text: From Performance to Print* (Bloomington: Indiana University Press, 1984), 88.

10. Victor Turner, *From Ritual to Theatre: The Human Seriousness of Play* (New York: Performing Arts Journal, 1982), 101. See also Turner's *The Anthropology of Performance* (New York: Performing Arts Journal, 1986).

11. For an excellent discussion of New Journalism, see David L. Eason, "The New Journalism and the Image-World: Two Modes of Organizing Experience," *Critical Studies in Mass Communication* 1 (March 1984): 51–65.

12. John Van Maanen, *Tales of the Field: On Writing Ethnography* (Chicago: University of Chicago Press, 1988), 102–3.

13. His work is most fully described in Craig Gingrich-Philbrook, "A Performance Artist's Discourse: Performance Studies and Fragments of Postmodernity" (Ph.D. diss., Southern Illinois University, Carbondale, 1994).

14. Elliot Linwood, "Stand Up Theory," *High Performance* 55 (fall 1991): 16.

15. Adrienne Rich, *What Is Found There: Notebooks on Poetry and Politics* (New York: Norton, 1993), 13.

16. Minh-ha, 28.

17. Tess Gallagher, "The Poem as Time Machine," *Claims for Poetry*, ed. Donald Hall (Ann Arbor: University of Michigan Press, 1982), 107.

18. Donald Revell, "Betraying the Silence," *American Poetry Review* 21 (September/October 1992): 17.

Acknowledgments

This book received its first delicate push at a research retreat in the summer of 1994 with several dear colleagues, James VanOosting (Seton Hall University), Nathan Stucky (Southern Illinois University), Elyse Pineau (Southern Illinois University), Tami Spry (St. Cloud State University), Sharon Bebout (Southeast Missouri State University), Sharon Taylor (Southwest College), and Craig Gingrich-Philbrook (Southern Illinois University). Since then, these colleagues have continued their gentle pushing. To them, I owe my sincere thanks. Others, too, have helped immensely in moving this project along, including Sheron Dailey (Indiana State University), Lesa Lockford (Centenary College), Jill Taft-Kaufman (Central Michigan University), Mary Hinchcliff-Pelias (Southern Illinois University), H. L. Goodall (University of North Carolina, Greensboro), Tracey J. Sobol-Hill (Southern Illinois University Press), Marie Maes (professional freelance copyeditor), and Tessa O. Pelias (Carbondale Community High School). To them, I also owe my sincere thanks.

Grateful acknowledgment is also made to Harcourt Brace for permission to reproduce selected lines from T. S. Eliot's "The Love Song of J. Alfred Prufrock." An earlier version of chapter 1 appeared as "An Autobiography of Performance in Everyday Discourse," *Journal of Dramatic Theory and Criticism* 8 (1994): 163–72, and a previous version of chapter 7 was published as "Confessions of an Apprehensive Performer," *Text and Performance Quarterly* 17 (1997): 25–32, the latter used by permission of the National Communication Association. Thanks as well to *San Fernando Poetry Journal* where my poem, "Border Crossing," first appeared and to the following for permission to use their names in connection with factual accounts in my discussion: Dacia Charlesworth, Craig Gingrich-Philbrook, Liz Gullickson-Tolman, Mary Hinchcliff-Pelias, Lesa Lockford, Gus M. Pelias, Gus M. Pelias Jr., Tessa O. Pelias, Keith Pounds, Anita Rich, and Tracy Stephenson.

Performing Every Day

1

An Ethnographic Autobiography of Performance in Everyday Life

To begin, start with a simple question: How can the performative in everyday discourse be described? Rule 1: Make sure the self is at the center of the report. Rule 2: Make sure the self is sufficiently in the background. Self-indulgence is not permitted. Being boring is even worse. To continue, find a label: autobiographic ethnography.

After asking my seven-year-old daughter to help me brainstorm for a solution to a family problem, she replies, "I would like to help but in my brain, it's a sunny day." We laugh in shared recognition.

To engage in an autobiographic ethnography is to enact the old aestheticism. It is to create a rhetorical dandy, who, as Geertz tells us, must more than anything else present an engaging persona, one who seduces readers into believing that they are in the company they wish to keep. The scholar as aesthete is nothing more than and nothing less than a negotiation of personality, an actor who turns life into art.

A colleague offers a course entitled "Teaching as Performance." The comparison, like teaching is an art, seems obvious. I stop to consider poet Al Young's lines:

> The face out there
> interacting with yours
> knows how to grin & play with its pen
> but misses the point so charmingly

and Theodore Roethke's strange fixation on poor dead Jane's neck curls.

Kevin Costner in his role of Robin Hood had another actor stand in for the scene in which his bottom is exposed. What does this do to the notion of presence and absence to call upon a stand-in butt?

3

I write a line, "Some ease in, tense." It serves as a beginning for a little poem that compares entering water with entering into relationships. The poem is finished, the line is gone, like orange, in Frank O'Hara's "Why I Am Not a Painter."

A friend described a time when she asked her daughter to tell her about a party she had just attended. Her daughter replied, "I can't. I haven't remembered it yet."

A sneeze. It evokes, if one were to work through just some of the "a's," argument, affirmation, awkwardness, assault, approval, aggravation, assiduity, awareness, applause, action, adoration, avoidance, assimilation, aggression, appreciation, authorization, anger, attention, appeasement, agitation, attack, adjudication, authentication, abhorrence, affinity, astonishment, apology, agony, adoration, assurance, alacrity, alignment, anxiety, anticipation, adjustment, affection, assistance, alienation, advice, annihilation, allegiance, adversity, altercation, amusement, admiration, ambivalence, ambiguity, admonishment, amenity, altruism, amazement, and autobiography.

Meaning is radically contingent.

A sneeze again. This time strategic, an action seeking audience. Its design is sympathy. Let's not forget who is feeling sick here.

These are confessions of an apprehensive performer. To confess demands an audience. Yet, to solicit an audience is to invite apprehension. It comes sure as the winter's sleet, slicing through all speech. I write in fear. I speak in fear. I cannot escape the other's gaze, the look that examines or discards like male lust. In their eyes, I read my sorry self. Like Prufrock, I have worried that "my hair is growing thin." I have "measured out my life in coffee spoons." I count my vita lines and go to bed.

An invitation comes to perform some of my poems. I'm given a few days to consider the offer. The opportunity is too alluring for my ego to refuse. I am seduced by the promise. But for two days I see poems shaking in my trembling hands.

Your hands shake. Your mouth feels dry. You sweat. You feel the rings form under your arms. Your voice quivers. Your eyes blur. You cannot focus. You're warm. Your knees lock. You begin to walk. You think you might fall. You fix your clothes. You put your hands in your pockets. Your pulse races. You're aware of the pounding of your heart.

Here are the words: stage fright, terror, nervousness, anxiety, reticence, shyness, fear, trepidation, dread, panic, agitated, uneasy, phobic, queasy, timid, distraught, scared.

Here are the academically correct words: communication apprehension.

Here are the politically correct words: communication disadvantaged.

Young Boy 1: I know how to spell "soldiers."
Young Boy 2: No you don't.
Young Boy 1: Yes I do! "Sahfirgtbvw."
Young Boy 2: Oh.

I am still spelling "soldiers."

There is a tradition: Charles Baudelaire, Filippo Tommaso Marinetti, Oscar Wilde, H. Norman Schwartzkopf, Anaïs Nin, Joseph Beuys, Madonna, Charles Bukowski, Ronald Reagan, Piero Manzoni, Walter Cronkite, Tom Wolfe. Is turning one's life into an art more than a marketing strategy? Is it genuine incarnation? Is it the individual answer to theatrical spectacle?

Madonna, truth or dare: Do you believe what you say? Are you genuine? Are you putting us on? Are you sincere? The cross hangs between your pointed breasts.

Freed from the burden of logical argument, I offer contingencies, random thoughts, tenuous connections, solipsistic references, feelings (petty and otherwise), personal impressions, selected notes, private confessions. The new burden: Hold interests, engage, be witty and startling, hold interests.

The postmodern mandate is the Sophists' proof.

Helen Hayes says she knew how to play a particular character when she remembered a Joseph Conrad line: "[S]he had the awesome power of intimacy."

I have been a victim to such power.

"Fly, fly" I say with W. S. Merwin, for I too "have always believed too much in words." Yes, I want to be seen as someone who knows poetry, or better, someone who uses poetry.

As I read the opening chapters of Michael Kirby's *A Formalist Theatre*, I watch his struggle toward a definition of theatre and acting. What to rule in; what to rule out. The boundary cases are always the most interesting. He argues that the key to theatre is intent, the intent to create an event that will affect an audience. Dinner is served.

A black man works the crowd in New York City: "Give to the United Negro Sausage Fund." Some laugh and he continues: "If you won't give to the UNSF, then give because it was a creative try." We all move on. So much for art.

A friend tells me the following story: A couple who had been married for fifty years were to be honored by their church. Just prior to the service, the priest identified three different times when they would be asked to do something. The husband became quite concerned that he wouldn't remember what to do when. In an effort to comfort him, the wife leaned over to pat his hand and said, "Don't worry, even those big Hollywood stars forget their lines sometimes." They don't need Kirby to know what theatre is.

What really happened was that the husband comforted the wife, not vice versa. Details may be changed to protect the genders. Details may be changed to protect ourselves. Details may be changed to protect me.

The Question: "I am an older woman coming back to school, and I would like to know what you can tell me about Public Speaking."
The Reply: "It is a course designed to help you prepare and deliver public speeches."
Imagined Reply: "You give speeches and make sure that you don't talk about baking tuna casserole for your demonstration speech."

So much for being politically correct.

If I get it, it ain't avant-garde. The avant-garde at the Lincoln Center is an oxymoron. The avant-garde exists on the margins. It knows what is at stake in rearranging the pieces. When we (or should I say, the bourgeoisie) understand, all is lost.

David Gordon's "Mysteries and What's So Funny?" was the first presentation of the fifth annual Serious Fun series at Lincoln Center's Tully Hall. I was only one of a handful of people wearing a coat and tie.

After buying a half-priced ticket ($37.50) in Times Square, I hear a man's plea for donations for the homeless. I am persuaded by the passion of his speech and drop a dollar into his box. The next day I hear his plea again and wonder if he is legitimate. I walk past. So much for art.

The liturgical debate concerning what substances should be used for communion is a question of representation. It is a semiotic debate: "grape juice/wine/blood" and "wafer/bread/body." Props count.

I enjoy telling the story of how my wife went out one day and bought herself a jeep, taking me completely by surprise. I am at my male best (or worst) in the telling. It makes for a good story, a moment in conversation that plays fairly well. It is, of course, a lie. We knew then and we know now what was and is happening. The fiction we allow is a shared public performance, a light comedy we stage periodically. All art is ideological.

This piece is about my performance in everyday interactions. Our interaction is a performance about alternatives to scholarly representation.

Scholarship and fiction are more than related; they are those incestuous cousins.

Once there was a man who wanted to tell a story. So he began, and as he spoke he wasn't sure if he was telling the story he wanted to tell. There were many tales he could tell, but he could only tell one at a time. He had picked a story to tell and had already begun to tell it when he wondered if it was the story he wanted to tell. Even more, he wasn't sure who was doing the telling. He wondered if it was really him who was speaking or if he was just a storyteller. He spoke more loudly, trying to find out, but he was still unsure. He held a mirror up to his face, but that didn't help either. He repeated what he had said; he tried whispering; he invited others to listen. Nothing helped. He wondered if anyone would believe the story he was telling and if they did believe, who were they believing. He wondered if he was telling the truth or if he would know if he wasn't. Then he thought about why he wanted to tell the story, and he began again. Once there was a man who . . .

Just making conversation, Clifton asked, "What are you working on these days?"

"Oh, a couple of things. The one I'm having the most fun with is a piece I'm calling 'An Autobiographic Ethnography of Performance in Everyday Discourse.'"

"Pretty loose use of the term 'ethnography,' isn't it?"

"I suppose so, but it does capture some things I like–doing fieldwork on oneself, acting as a participant/observer. You know, that kind of thing."

"Why do you think," Clifton said, becoming even more suspicious of the project, "that people would care about you as a subject? I mean, what do you offer the reader by exploring your performance in everyday life?"

"I hope the piece moves beyond a simple self-report. The piece is really about modes of proof."

"Well, good luck with it," said Clifton, escaping to his office.

I put *Les Miserables* on the Walkman and turn the volume to ten. I sing. I orchestrate. It is a religious experience. What bleeding heart liberal can resist?

My daughter shows me her day's work: a puppet made from a lunch bag, arms colored and glued, one placed near the hip and the other exiting from the ear. The eyes, nose, and mouth are best described as variations on a circle. All are in red crayon, seriously contrasting with the orange hair. The puppet, spotted with extra glue, has been oddly folded and stuffed in my daughter's lunch box for the passage home. I think I detect some grape jelly on the forehead. "It's wonderful, darling," I say.

> Between fact one and fact two is reading.
>
> Between reading one and reading two is interpretation.
>
> Between interpretation one and interpretation two is understanding.
>
> Between understanding one and understanding two is dialogue.
>
> Between dialogue one and dialogue two is truth.
>
> Between truth one and truth two is presence.
>
> Between presence one and presence two is performance.

I can best describe my performance behavior by thinking of a continuum from simple action to staged action. The simple action end of the continuum acknowledges that I can view all of my behavior as performance. In this sense, to do is to perform. Or, to adapt the familiar claim of one cannot not communicate, I can say that I cannot not perform. There is often a difference, though, between those acts I simply do and those acts I do when conscious that I am being observed. Awareness of spectator presence often alters my action. I feel a pressure to do the action right. The pressure increases even more when I invite others to focus upon my behavior. When I do such actions as taking the floor in informal conversation or calling attention to some physical feat, I establish performer/audience roles. I also change the dynamic when I suggest to my audience that by focusing on me, they will encounter the aesthetic. I tell stories, jokes, puns; I mimic others for comic effect; I make mock threats; I tease with transparent lies. In short, I engage in a myriad of conversational behaviors that I offer as aesthetic. At times, moving further on the continuum, I offer public presentations, created for anticipated audiences. I lecture to my classes, give speeches on various occasions, read papers at academic conferences, and so on. These, too, are potentially aesthetic acts. Marking the end of the continuum are my staged actions, those events typically considered theatre. I usually present these actions in designated performance spaces and frame them as theatrical events.

This scheme is a phenomenological report. It tells of my sense of everyday performance, my sense of what actions are more or less theatrical for me. It empowers spectators, making my own and others' intent fundamental and establishing the communicative frame essential. It forgets, as I do in my everyday life, that I am bound by my culture and history.

A doctoral student comes by who I have not seen for several years. I am both glad to see her and protective of the time she might demand. We give each other a cautious hug. So much for teaching as an art.

Account 1:

He has not escaped his gender. He is a white North American male doing the best he knows how. He makes mistakes; he offends, but never intentionally. He has changed significantly.

Account 2:

He has all the typical biological drives—he eats, sleeps, makes love, and so on. These drives, as many anthropological studies have led us to expect, become evident in more or less elaborate rituals. Eating, for example, demands the execution of certain rules of preparation and consumption. He also goes about his business in keeping with the familiar white North American male behavior. He is loud, takes up considerable space, and acts as if the world is his. Like others of his kind, he holds a position of power and has been known to use it. He knows enough to appear sensitive to those who have been marginalized but goes about his affairs without much real concern. He lives in suburbia and manicures his lawn. When he speaks, he expects others to listen without interruption. He has been known to hold forth, to offer truth, and to silence others. He has little regard for . . .

Account 3:

When we speak, I am aware that he is a large male, but he carries himself in a gentle manner. He likes women, and I never feel intimidated when we talk. We have had some rich conversations. Most often, he plays the role of devil's advocate, and I respond. We engage in the academic game very well. We follow its rules, privilege its logic, trust its values. We knead ideas together.

Account 4:

He's an ass.

To end, finish with a simple question: Has the story been told? Rule 1: Ask if it was worth telling. Rule 2: See if the dandy's clothes are wrinkled. Rule 3: Try again. The greatest dishonesty is the illusion of disclosure. To continue, provide a summary: This performance is an ethnographic account presented on behalf of myself in the hope of some understanding. To finalize, stop with T. S. Eliot's line: "But I gotta use words when I talk to you."

2

Naming Men: The Business of Performing Manly

This essay is about naming, about getting things out. It will see who measures up. It wants to establish what counts, to check the score, to figure all the angles. It wants to flex its muscles. It wants to show its stuff. It will strut its time upon the page. It will twist each idea to suit its purposes. It will win the day. This is, so they say, a manly thing to do, a manly way to be.

Webster, you are out. You have been named.

You've got all the words, so how could you define us as individuals "possessing in high degree the qualities distinctive of manhood (as courage, strength, vigor)"? How could you say that manhood equals the "manly qualities" of "courage, bravery, resolution" and add "honor, gallantry, nobility, forcefulness, daring, boldness, tenacity, self-reliance, potency" in your thesaurus? How could you state masculine is "having the qualities distinctive of or appropriate to a male: virile, robust, manly"?

Robert Bly, you are out. You have been named.

So sad for a poet who once could count small-boned bodies. Come on Robert,

> Let's count the bodies over again.
>
> If we could only make the bodies manly
> The penis size doubled
> We could hang the wimps with our ropes in the
>   moonlight!
>
> If we could only make the bodies manly
> Maybe we could number them
> As they march over their sons following you into the
>   woods.

1. Be able to lift your own body weight.
2. Never be the last player to be picked.
3. Make gobs of money.
4. Talk like a man, preferably one from Mars.
5. Rule the world.
6. Don't be afraid of the dark.
7. Know the scores.
8. Know how to score.
9. Fix everything.
10. Look down when kissing.
11. Be prepared.
12. Wash regularly.

play perfectly—both of you coming on court in full costume, acting as if you were playing hard, knocking Barney over until he was in shambles, and walking off with Barney, arm in arm, to his theme song without spitting on anyone.

Davy Crockett, you are out. You have been named.

Defend until the last man is standing. Defend as if dirt were more meaningful than death. Defend as if such words as "honor" and "valor" were not an ideological fiction. Defend until the last man says no more.

Frank, you are out. You have been named.

You sat at your lover's funeral accused, named from the pulpit. The man of God pointed his holy finger directly at you in his prayer that Armageddon would soon arrive so that your sin of loving another man would be swept away in God's forgiving grace. You listened out of respect for your lover's wishes and for his family. You listened because you had no choice. Unlike those of us sitting in the back who became angrier and angrier but said nothing, you listened with gentle understanding and forgiveness. With tears, with the weight of losing the one you loved, and with the HIV virus running in your veins, you were a good man.

After the graveside burial, our services began. Six of us gathered in his name. With magic markers, we wrote messages to him on helium balloons and watched them float beyond sight: "We'll miss you." "We won't forget you." "Remember us." In the silence of that moment, he was present, handsome and golden. Then, we circled, arm in arm, leaned forward until our heads almost touched, and said his name. He was a good man.

Chiefs of Staff, you are out. You have been named.

You are so strong that I'll bet you could scatter whole armies by one swing of your scrotum. Don't let the soft boys in. You are so big, I'll bet you could rape villagers after each U.S. victory. Don't let the soft boys in. You stand so erect, I'll bet you could do dead corpses in your sleep. Don't let the soft boys in. That's why you are the Chiefs of Staff.

Craig, you are out. You have been named.

You showed me a photograph of you during a recent march on Washington for gay rights. In the background are thousands who came in support. But also slightly behind and to the side of you is a man who, if one can judge from appearances, is looking at you with disdain. His contempt seemed to find you because you stopped to pose. You were a convenient target. You were a symbol of all that had gone wrong. Smiling for the camera's click, you were unaware of the presence of such hate. But after the photograph froze the moment, you pointed to that man and said, "That's who I want to reach in my performance work. I want to include him."

William Shakespeare, you are out. You have been named.
She had you Willie. She had you in her hands. She reduced you to those sniffling lyrics, those syrupy sonnets. She turned you into mush—a mere word master, murmuring soft nothings. She kept you from listening to yourself.

> All this the world well knows; yet none knows well
> To shun the heaven that leads men to this hell.

Or are you writing to another man?

Dick Butkus, you are out. You have been named.
You were the ultimate man of the Sunday wars. Your trade was violence, physical punishment, bodily harm. You played with abandon, with no care for your own physical being. Instinct drove you. Passion controlled you. You lived in that pure moment when forces collide. It was raw energy, spoken in the simplest terms. We came to our feet just watching you. Others have come to take your place.

Peewee Herman, Hugh Grant, Charlie Sheen, George Michael, and Woody Allen, you are out. You have been named.
As men, let's judge these men. Let's say what is right as if we never would do such things, as if we never had such desires, as if we would feel righteous after throwing our stones. Let's put them on trial as if there is a difference in doing and getting caught. Let's make them apologize publicly as if apologies might substitute for who we are.

Jesse Helms, you are out but are not worth naming.
We know you for what you are, a self-anointed, lord god on earth who condemns all who are not made in your image. May God forgive you.

Tim Allen, you are out. You have been named.
Grunt for me, Tim. Grunt for all the times I thought I had it right. Grunt for all the times I've had it wrong. Grunt for all the times I've needed to stand up and say, "This is who I am. This is who I am."

Narcissus, you are out. You have been named.
We caught you looking, admiring yourself, gazing for your pleasure. We should have known then that the male gaze has no interest beyond itself, that it has no Echo.

Naming Men

Real men, you are out. You have been named.

Names that are reminders of what we are not: Bruce Lee, Arnold Schwarzenegger, Spiderman, Bruce Jenner, Kirk Douglas, Burt Reynolds, James Bond, Clark Gable, Michael Jordan, Ernest Hemingway, Humphrey Bogart, Johnny Cash, Richard Burton, Superman, Clint Eastwood, Hulk Hogan, Rambo, Jean-Claude Van Damme, Tarzan, John Wayne, Pat Riley, Rocky, Omar Sharif, Popeye, Gary Cooper, General Schwartzkopf, Mickey Spillane, Charlton Heston, Daniel Boone, Batman, Steven Seagal, Harrison Ford, Tommy Lee Jones, Marlon Brando, Wesley Snipes, Errol Flynn, Mike Hammer, and on and on.

Names that are reminders of what we are: Mike Tyson, Howard Stern, Mark Fuhrman, Billy Carter, Daryl Strawberry, Heinrich Himmler, David Koresh, Newt Gingrich, Tom Arnold, Prince Charles, Michael Jackson, Tiny Tim, Pete Rose, Snoop Doggie Dog, Jerry Lee Lewis, Elvis Presley, Norman Bates, Jim Bakker, Richard Nixon, the artist formerly known as Prince, Charles Manson, O. J. Simpson, Ronald Reagan, Al Capone, Jim Belushi, Attila the Hun, Jeffrey Dahmer, Charlie Chaplin, Oliver North, and on and on.

Tim Miller, you are out. You have been named.

Tim, you've got charm, standing onstage nude, talking to your penis. You've got balls; I've seen them. You've got a right to speak to all who will listen and to all who need to hear. Tim, I went with you into your dream volcano and found gay desire simply desire. I found your desire no different from my own. I found your desire remarkably unremarkable.

Van Gogh, you are out. You have been named.

I've known your "Starry Night," with its seductive swirls, your "Olive Grove," with its blue branches, and your "Prisoners' Courtyard," with its circle of cellmates. But I turn again to your "Self-portrait with Bandaged Ear" knowing your self-mutilation allowed you to work. You look at us with your steady green eyes as if to say, "What else would you have me do?"

Mel Gibson, you are out. You have been named.

Mel, you could have been of use. You could have been an example. You could have been the Braveheart of the Care Bears, the gentle lion who offers rainbows of love in his Care Bear cousin calls. But you chose to be a different Braveheart, a warrior, driven by injustice, to maim and kill. For you are the ultimate man, conquering all, from women to lords. Led by those hollow signifiers, revenge and bravery, you fight in the name of freedom while you oppress.

You bed your adversary's daughter-in-law and expect to be our hero? Keep it in your pants. We do not trust you. You avenge your wife's murder with murder and believe we'll celebrate your virtue. Revenge owns the fool's heart. We do not trust you. You go charging with savage abandon into another army and assume that we will follow. Bravery is a weak cousin to talk. We do not trust you. And perhaps saddest of all, you picture a gay man as your antithesis and think you're the man we want to be. We know better than to believe that to be gay is to move with a band of merry men whose only interests are in bellying up to one another. We know better than to believe that to be gay is to be ineffectual, unable to marry who you wish, unable to protect those you love, unable to confront your father, unable to lead others, unable to relate to women, unable to be a man. We do not trust you. And we do not trust ourselves.

I too have felt the demands of bravery, in the pressure to stand up, as the saying goes, for myself and have found myself sitting on the sideline. I sat in my adolescent years after challenging a kid who was spitting on passengers as they left the bus. "You shouldn't do that," I mustered. "Do you want to make something of it?" came the reply. "No." I sat in my car without fighting back as a high school acquaintance punched me three times for dating "his girl." I sat shaking in my Vietnam boots as rockets exploded around the compound. From the moment of my fifth-grade wrestling match with Billy Davenport that landed me in the mud, fighting seemed silly. So, I am a coward. I am no John Wayne, no Rambo, no Braveheart. I will cross a city street to avoid potential danger. I will sneak quietly from a barroom brawl. I will slide through the night in silence. I will pretend that I wouldn't.

I too have felt the lure of revenge. I've wanted to get even when I've felt I was done wrong. But my method is not the ax but the cutting tongue. Usually, I work quickly—a word here, a look there, a gesture placed at just the right moment. Behind the back, I slice, mince, and puree. I can serve up my enemies with amenities. But I will not do bodily harm to another. My mode is only psychological.

I too have felt the power of heterosexual privilege as I laughed at gay jokes, as I witnessed scenes on television and film of heterosexual desire displayed for my pleasure, as I walked down the street holding my wife's hand without fear. No one snickers when I smile at another man. No one smirks when I go out with the "boys." No one spews obscenities when I'm out with the person I love. And I have felt subjected to the power of heterosexual oppression.

I chose to see *Braveheart* knowing that such scripts oppress, making us all subject to the horrific hegemony of the manly. So why did I go? That I might fantasize through my inadequacy, that I might live up to the cultural code, that I might become more like a man?

Mel Gibson, I do not like you, and I do not like me. I am your weak partner, seduced by what I reject in you. In naming you, I name me. I am only a milder and more insidious version of you.

Walt Whitman, you are out. You have been named.

I want your song, but instead I sing the Body defective. I come with decaying teeth and sour breath. I know my skin where the moles were scraped and where they grow. I remember where the scabs filled with pus and where the boils were lanced. I've felt my body's spit fly from my mouth, my snot run down my lip, my phlegm driven from my lungs. I've seen my blood.

I've seen the Body defective, mangled from birth, from war, from age so that it could not help itself. I've seen its deadly diseases add tubes, bags, and machines like new body parts. I've seen it drugged and mugged. I've seen it rape and kill in the name of its pleasure. I've seen it cry.

Touched, I've watched it freeze, watched it cringe. I've watched it alone, fondling itself. I've watched it hoping for contact, hoping for your song.

Brother, you are out. You have been named.

Builder of buildings, I claim you. You are foundational. You give me structure and support. Brick by brick, you created me. Beam by beam, you developed me. Nail by nail, you secured me. You live in my house without even knowing. You are my architect.

Dad, you are out. You have been named.

We share the same name, not the exact moniker as my older brother (your junior image), but exact enough to claim a heritage, Greek, mixed with a bland, middle-class, American sauce. We break bread together, you at the head of the table but never using the authority of your position. Your strategy is not based in laws but wishes, wishes we want to heed. So it must be said, first, we are named under the name of love. And as I live my life as a man, I remember you before me, always present, always a reminder.

I remember your perfect Greek body with its Michelangelo muscles, possessing a strength I would never match. I watched that perfect body lift with ease cases of carrots, cranberry, and coffee onto a delivery truck, toy with my brother and me as we arm wrestled on the living room floor, and stop a fight after a football game by holding the arms of a man determined to swing. That perfect Greek body isn't perfect anymore, with its accumulation of years, with its aches and pains, with its cancer.

I remember your brother, who, on the eve before I left for Vietnam, said, "Every boy should get a chance to fight in the war of his generation." I wanted no such chance, and I wanted to say so. But instead, I looked at my wife and my two-week-old son and knew that for the privilege of "fighting in the war of my generation" I would lose them both,

17

Benedictine University Library
Mesa Campus

as I did, in the years to come. I also looked at you who did not fight in the war of your generation listen with guilt as your brother spoke.

I remember cars, the company car I drove into the family car, which pushed into the living room like a strange metal beast, on my first driving lesson on my fourteenth birthday and you apologizing to me as if it were your fault. I remember the big 1962 Chevy, big enough for those beginning adolescent urges, that you gave me as my first car. I remember us both standing in front of our old smoke-spewing Oldsmobile without a clue of what to do. I remember that you found a used prophylactic in the Ford on your way to church and that you were convinced (and I must admit it was my sixteen-year-old wish) it held my semen. It was the only time you didn't believe me when I spoke the truth.

I remember the time you gave to me to support, to connect. We were together that night on the River Queen when you hit for seventy-five dollars on the machines with your first coin and we played the night away, giggling and drinking. We were together for your father's funeral, your hand resting on my shoulder while tears rolled down your cheeks. We were together, week after week, slugging away on the golf course, cursing and laughing, teasing and boasting, knowing we were sharing dreams beyond any game. These were lessons to be learned, lessons in the making of a man.

I remember when your Graves' disease struck, blurring your vision, holding your eyes always open. But you were never a Tiresias; with dimmed sight, you just saw less. There was no irony. But you drove the streets, hit your golf balls, and turned on television as if you could see as well as ever. You have always lived not with a soothsayer's eye into the future but in the present. And it is here in the present I want to hold you, always near, always with your eyes open.

When I was a teenager, you would say to me, "You can't burn a candle at both ends." But that is how you lived your life, and I've always been attracted to that image, enjoying the dual flame and anticipating the potential danger as the wax burns away the ends. Dad, our candle is burning. We have been holding it in the middle too long. Watch, I'm blowing out an end now to keep you here longer.

My son, you are out. You have been named.

All children are born in promise, born in hope. But when promise and hope fade, blood may thicken or thin. At two, I held you knowing a broken marriage would keep us apart. I looked down at you that night, sleeping, and felt the loss. At ten, after years of visits, I still thought of you as mine. I moved to be near you. At fifteen, it began to happen. You seemed more your stepfather's child than mine. You took on his traits, ones I could not abide. At twenty, I only hear from you when you need money.

We try to pretend otherwise. Our blood thins because of the lies we tell, because of the years apart, because of who we are.

Boys cannot escape their fathers' hold. Memory is my father's friend. Memory is my son's curse. Now he is a man.

Men, we are out. We have been named.

Blessed and cursed by our attractions, we are the fools of our own making. We do not know how to reach beyond ourselves. We learn as we stumble on.

> Between the pulling in and the pushing away, falls the pain.
> Between the pain and the pleasure, falls the desire.
> Between the desire and its fulfillment, falls the anticipation.
> Between the anticipation and the first touch, falls love.

Ron, you are out. You have been named.

So, you want to know if you measure up? Think about that relationship when your lover gave you a spear, then an ax, and finally a gun. Think about how at parties she would inch next to him like a snail, ready to suck on. Think about when you returned from a convention and you both lied about not sleeping with someone else.

You want to know if you are measuring up? Consider how you fall asleep watching the ten o'clock news, only to be awakened by your own snoring. Remember how you failed to put in the screens after a day's work or how you burned up your third lawn mower by forgetting to put in oil. Remember, you can't keep the National and American Leagues straight. Remember, you'd rather be listening to the talk of women than to the stories of men.

You want to know if you are measuring up? You cannot count those who you've once hurt. You cannot remember those who were once friends. You cannot name those who you've once loved.

You want to know if you are measuring up? Your body thickens, your fingers swell, and your hair begins to thin. You straighten your eyebrows and clip your ear hairs. You find this funny rather than sad. Aging, you have little time to measure up. Remember how you listened to two friends describe their husbands' bedroom behavior and felt they could have been describing you:

> "I don't like it when he . . ."
> "It makes my skin crawl when he . . ."
> "I hate it when he . . ."

There is so much you can do wrong, so much you do without knowing.

You want to know if you are measuring up when you look in a mirror and want to turn away. Your image surprises. Your image depresses. By design, you avoid mirrors. You don't know how to look. You don't know what you're afraid to see.

You should have known if you were measuring up when you tried to measure if you were measuring up. Measuring, as they say, is the province of men. You should have known when you wanted to give an accounting, when you wanted to name. You should have known when you reached this point without an answer.

3

Performing in the Classroom

You arrive a few minutes early on the first day. You look around but don't see anyone you know, just a few familiar faces but no one you think of as a friend. You take a seat by the window, not too close to the front of the class, yet not too far back. You pull your notebook from your book bag and leave the books you bought for the course resting snugly against your outrageous book bill for the semester. You write on the top of your first page: Introduction to Performance Studies. You want to look ready. You know how to act like a good student.

You enter right on the hour. You wanted to get there a few minutes ahead, but someone grabbed you as you were leaving your office. You are nervous, despite having taught this course many times before, despite having everything prepared for the class, despite having practiced saying everyone's name on the grade sheet. You write your name on the board and, pointing with your chalk, announce: "This is Introduction to Performance Studies, and this is who I am. Is everyone in the right place?" Two male students get up in the back and exit. You wave bye, acting a bit silly but thinking that too many men in a performance class is a sure formula for disaster. The class seems evenly split between men and women. You are pleased.

You watch him enter the room. He's dressed in jeans and a bright tie. He's big—tall, a little chunky, and tanned. He puts his stuff on the desk, and you see that you've bought the right book. You are pleased. After introducing himself, he begins to call the roll. You hate it when teachers try to make something of everyone's name: "Brandon. Are you related to Professor Brandon who teaches in Biology?" "Papolis sounds like a good Greek name. Do you speak any Greek?" "Smith. I'll bet I pronounced that one right." When he gets to you, he asks, "Were you in one of the MFA shows the Theatre Department did last semester?" You simply answer, "No." You are told you look familiar. Twenty minutes after the hour, he has finally finished calling everyone's name. You get a syllabus and turn to the assignment page. You want to know just what you'll have to do in here. You scan: three performances, two papers, two exams. What are these performances?

You have a love/hate relationship with first days. You love the promise, the starting over, the excitement. You hate having to prove again to those resistant bodies that what you want to talk about is worth talking about. You hate laying out the rules: "You must come to class, particularly on performance days." "If you miss your own scheduled time for performance, you cannot make it up unless you have a documented medical excuse." "You must attend two performances outside of class from this list of scheduled events." You hate the questions that are designed to discover how little one has to do. You describe in detail all the course assignments, paying particular attention to the required performance work.

You raise your hand to ask for clarification: "We select any three poems from this handout to perform, right? But what do you mean by 'perform'?" You listen as he turns your question into a question for the class. When he returns to you ten minutes later, you still don't know what he wants. "Does that help at all?" You nod, not wanting to admit you're not quite getting it. You nod, noticing that the time for the class is at an end. You nod, wondering if you should drop.

You smile, feeling you gave her a rich response to a question that has no one-two-three answer. You are pleased that you managed to get the class to note that performance occurs in everyday life, in rituals, in theatre spaces. You smile, thinking that this group seems responsive. You like the kid wearing the Cubs' cap but cannot remember his name. You are glad to have Jenny, the carefully dressed and groomed sorority woman who will do B+/A- work all semester in her eager and serious preprofessionalism. You're sure she is a public relations major. You smile, amazed that the allotted time for the class is over. "Next time," you say, "we'll really get down to work." You watch as they flood your desk with questions that could have been answered during class.

You decide to try the class one more day. You listen as he spends the entire class presenting what he calls "a working definition of performance studies." You know you will have to memorize this definition for the exam, so you jot it down in your notebook. You listen as he begins talking about art. You almost raise your hand before you realize that no matter what someone says, he will turn it around. You wonder if all teachers enjoy making students feel like they don't know what they're saying. You write, "Art can't be defined," but have a notion that isn't what he wants you to get out of all this mumbo jumbo.

You are giving one of your favorite lectures, one you've given many times before and always enjoy. It's jazzy and filled with information you want them to have. It always gets a good discussion going. You are coming to your favorite part. After getting them to share their definitions of art, you tell them that you're going to create a work of art that will meet their criteria. You get a piece of paper, hold it in front of you, crumble it as you scream in agony, and drop it to the floor. You love how they always jump when you scream. You love turning to them and asking, "Is that art? It fits all your criteria, doesn't it?"

You almost fell out of your seat when he yelled. You think the man must be possessed. You watch hands go up as half your classmates say what he did is art and the other half say it isn't. You are with those who say it isn't. You see his next question coming: "Why do you think it is or isn't?" You wonder, "Why do you think we should care?" You just know that you want more from art than an earache. You start to laugh when you tell your friend about it during lunch. Your friend wants to know if the teacher thought it was art. You don't know. You'd drop but the two other classes you were considering would mess up your schedule.

You leave feeling the class is off to a good start. You were able to stir things up a bit, able to get a number of them talking. You had them thinking about art in some fairly sophisticated ways. You now worry, however, that by giving various conceptions of art, you've opened the relativism door, a door the students seem too comfortable entering. You tried to slam that door shut, but you doubt if everyone was following you. You worry, too, that the discussion was too loose, too abstract, too open ended. You worry that they won't be able to handle an essay question on the various definitions of art on the midterm exam. You know the next session with them will be quite different. You're planning to lead the class in a series of body exercises.

You are among those who giggle nervously when he starts class by saying, "Today, I want to work on your bodies." Following instructions, you put away your notebook, help push the desks to the back of the room, and come forward. You listen to him talk about why body training is important for the performer but doubt whether you need any such thing to get through this class. You see his hand reach out for yours: "If you don't mind, I'd like to use your body to show the class how to do the first exercise." You take his hand instinctively, thinking "I do mind. I do mind." You'd rather know what you'll have to do before going up front. He instructs you to turn sideways to the class and just relax with your hands at your side. He begins tapping up and down from your elbow to your neck. After making sure everyone sees what he is doing, he rocks you slightly, holding your shoulders. You recognize how this might reduce tension.

You wonder if introducing students to a few body exercises throughout the semester accomplishes much. You enjoy the different feel of class on those days. You believe that most students not only have fun on these days but also discover how body training is central to the performer's craft. You know, too, the resistance. You watch the students who try to remain unnoticed by hiding in the back, who cannot let themselves fully participate, who spend their time self-consciously wondering if they are being watched. Working with the body takes away familiar student scripts. You proceed, however, as if asking people to make monster faces in front of one another is commonplace. You operate as if telling beginning students to experience an imaginative bubble filled with champagne is innocuous. You act as if pulling a shy student in front of the class to demonstrate how to do an exercise is sound pedagogical practice. You end class on the minute: "Some of you seemed reluctant or disinclined to participate. What does that say about you? What does that suggest about you as a developing performer?"

Gathering your things, you answer in your head: "It says I don't much like making a fool of myself. It says I just want my B out of this class and I want to be left alone. It says I have no intention of ever becoming a performer, so you can go train someone else. It says I resent being yanked into volunteering and then being told I was hesitant to participate. It says I'm dreading my first performance."

You've generated a fifteen-page handout of short poems, none over eight lines and most around four lines long. You require students to stage any three poems for their first performance assignment. You are chagrined by how many students select the few two line poems. You will cut them from the list when you use this assignment again. You are discouraged by the number of students who have trouble remembering their lines. You are disappointed by the lack of effort and imagination. You are frustrated, disheartened, angry. No one, it seems, has listened. Even so, you always welcome first performances. They provide something concrete, a genuine starting place. They point to those who are committed, to those who are thinking, to those who have talent. They signal promise.

Waiting for your turn, you cannot focus on the first two performers. You are reciting your poems over and over in your head. You were pleased with how you performed them for your rehearsal partner last night, but you weren't nervous then. You hear your name, and you are on. You get through all of your poems without forgetting a word. Only in your second do you slightly stumble over a phrase. You even present the last with some intensity, like you practiced. You return to your seat dazed and amazed that it's over. You think you did well. You await the verdict.

You want to be encouraging. Usually, you can find something positive to say about every performance. Usually, you know exactly what is needed. Usually, you can get them back on their feet and, with a few directorial suggestions, work wonders. But when you get to the third performer from that day, you can't remember what she did. You are embarrassed. You look at your notes and see the poems she performed. You note that you've written "adequate" under memorization, but that is of little help. You have a vague sense that all of the pieces sounded alike. You ask the performer to identify how any one of the poems is clearly distinct from one of the others. She offers a good answer that allows you the out you need: "Let's see if we can play on that contrast more fully in performance. Come on up." That night you still cannot remember her presentation. You write a few cliché critical comments that you are sure are safe and give her a B-.

You have to wait until the end of the performance round before you get your grade. Your eyes quickly scan the sheet until they land on B-. You are satisfied but had hoped for higher. You read: "Play on the inherent tensions within and between your selections." You knew he wanted you to make your pieces sound different, but you are not sure what he means by "work for greater complexity with your characterizations." You are pleased that he thinks this was a good first performance. You begin to think about your next one, due in just two weeks.

You've found that many students do their best performance work during the personal narrative round. Maybe it's because they are telling their own stories, maybe because memorization seems less intimidating when they try to remember something they've written, or maybe because they have a need to share aspects of their lives. You remember from previous classes the student who sang a Vietnamese folk song as she told of her voyage to the United States, the one who described how he lost his hand in a coal-mining accident, and the one who admitted that the summer she worked as a lifeguard in Disney World, she peed down the super slide. You're delighted the round is starting.

You're glad you're not scheduled until the fourth performance day. That gives you another week to practice and a chance to see what others will do. You watch the performances of the first day—nothing remarkable until the last one. A woman, you think her name is Marge, discloses how she was sexually abused by her father. She tells how she would awake to find her father mauling her and how her mother would not believe a word she said. As the performance goes on, you observe her getting more and more distressed. You don't think you are witnessing a performance anymore. By the end of the piece, she is sobbing, whimpering. No one applauds. She is just sitting onstage crying. You and a few others move to her onstage and take her in your arms. After some time, you notice the instructor pull away from the group onstage and say, "That's enough for today. See you on Wednesday."

You are writing a letter of recommendation for a former student when Marge arrives at your office door. "Come on in, Marge." "I won't take much of your time," she begins. "I just wanted you to know that everything I said yesterday wasn't true. I made it all up." You are shocked, shaken, and then skeptical. You find her first performance more convincing than this one. "Do you think I should tell the class?" she asks. "If you would like to do that, we can take some time next class."

You are surprised when Marge returns to class on Wednesday. You listen as the instructor announces that Marge wants a few minutes to speak before performances begin. She says: "I want to thank everyone who was so nice to me after my performance. That's why I need to say that the story I told was just a story. None of it was true." You are stunned. You feel betrayed. From the back of the room, Jeff blurts out, "You mean your father didn't abuse you?" "That's right," she states adamantly, "I was never abused." You watch her fingers twist a paper clip. You study her face, hoping to know what to believe. Jeff fumbles on, "All that crying and stuff was just an act?" "Yes, it was just a performance."

Turning to you, she excuses herself from class: "Sorry, I can't stay today." She scoops up her book bag and is gone. You know everyone needs to talk. You listen as people express their feelings of confusion, anger, and sadness. You discuss how personal narratives may trouble easy distinctions between theatrical and interpersonal frames. You note how "truth" may have little relationship to actuality. You remind everyone that performance, by definition, places the self at risk. You feel this was an important session. When your next class list arrives, you see that Marge has dropped.

You continue working on your piece. You decided to share the story of your grandmother giving you the family ring when she was dying of cancer. As you rehearse the piece, you find yourself becoming upset over your grandmother's death. You had thought that you were through mourning. Each time you go through the story, you seem to sink in the memory of your grandmother. You cannot tell the story without feeling the loss. This story has become increasingly meaningful to you. It's become a way of paying tribute to a wonderful woman. You are deeply hurt when the theatre major, Steven, says during the critique that your performance was too sentimental, that it sounded like a Hallmark card.

You agree with the critique but decide to focus on the student's development as a performer. You remark on her increased ease onstage, her control of the material, her clear sense of attitude. You suggest that the ending might work better if, instead of struggling to take the ring off to show the audience, she were simply to look down at it. You will write a careful note on her critique form that addresses the sentimentality issue. You will act with sensitivity and sympathy as you give her a B for the performance. You will also give Jeff a C– for his performance that had him miming kissing and fondling his woman friend as he told of their first date. And you will give Jenny an A– for her well-rehearsed story of her sorority initiation ceremony that went awry. You will continue grading, dreading the impact grades will have when you return both their exams and performance critiques on the same day.

You learned one thing for sure from the last round: Don't tell people how you really feel. It didn't work out for Marge, and it didn't work out for you. Your feelings about your grandmother are more important to you than this class. You read again: "I appreciate your deep feelings over the loss of your grandmother. To help us see her more vividly, you might consider telling us about particular moments when your grandmother was 'the most caring person in the world.' In other words, instead of remaining in the abstract, consider showing us, through specific details, moments that were especially telling about your grandmother, much like you do when you tell about getting the ring. Is 'The Most Caring Person in the World' a good title for your narrative?" You still resent him telling you how you should have shared your feelings. They are your feelings to share. You still resent your feelings being given a grade, a B. You are, though, beginning to have some sense of what he might mean when you get your exam back: a 72! You shove your exam and critique in your book bag and, exasperated and confused, leave class thinking, "What does he expect!"

You're glad you waited until the end of the hour to give their exams and critiques back. You hate seeing the effect—the anger and frustration, the disappointment and hostility. Even after years of this tense ritual, you remain amazed how their bodies sag, how the room gains weight, how they turn on you. After dealing with the students who want to argue about how you graded their exam, you're pleased to escape even though you are off to a mandatory sexual harassment workshop. On your way, you think of Micha, the Japanese student whose shoulder you touched as you moved through the tight rows of desks to get to the back of the room. You think of Marge who you hugged after her performance. You think of Chris who you used to demonstrate the tapping exercise. You think of Steven whose back you patted as you told him what a fine performance he did. You don't want such possible interactions taken away. By the end of the workshop, you decide you're unwilling to change your behavior, even if it might be misinterpreted.

A week later, you see him approaching you during the intermission of *Live, Nude, and on Stage*, a show you are required to see that presents strippers' thoughts about the business. You both note that you're enjoying the show. You are surprised when he says, "Since your last performance, you've seemed a little upset. Is everything okay?" You start to say everything is fine but blurt out: "I guess I was angry over how everyone responded to my last performance." You talk throughout the intermission. Squeezing your hand, he ends the conservation by saying, "Again, I'm deeply sorry if anything I said was hurtful." You go back into the theatre feeling better about the class. You're shocked to learn how much money strippers can make.

You're glad you had a chance to talk with her. You welcome the reminder of how vulnerable performers can feel, of how devastating a single comment can be, of how negative responses, no matter how carefully stated, carry ten times the weight of positive remarks. You look forward to having the old Chris, the attentive, questioning one, back in class. As you attempt to cover metrics, from jump rope songs, to nursery rhymes, to poems, you could use someone who isn't afraid to admit when she isn't getting it. You question if metrics is worth introducing in the beginning class. You wonder why students typically do their worst work with their third performances.

You selected Anne Sexton's poem, "The Starry Night," to perform. You've worked hard rehearsing but realize that you should have looked up the Van Gogh painting, when he brings a copy of it to class "just in case anybody hadn't seen it." You remember seeing the footnote in your anthology pointing to Van Gogh's "Starry Night" but didn't bother to look it up. He asks you if you considered having the painting present during your performance. You admit that you hadn't seen the painting before today. He begins discussing what its presence might add and might diminish. You feel embarrassed. You are surprised when you read on your

28

critique: "You had a nice feel for how the speaker is seduced by the images in the painting." You are also surprised by the grade: B+. You are most surprised, however, when he returns from a convention in New York City and gives you a postcard of Van Gogh's "Starry Night."

You made the best case for literature that you could. During the round, you gave them texts on related themes to ones they selected. You copied for them favorite poems of yours by authors they chose. You traced allusions by reading from the *Iliad* and the Bible and by showing a Van Gogh painting. You displayed your pleasure in literature, noting compelling images, reciting lush lines, pausing on powerful passages. You treated their texts as sacred, holy objects to be revered. You treated them as candy, scrumptious edibles sweet to the taste. You treated them as truth, and they treated them as a task. They forgot words; they dropped lines; they missed the point. But you persisted, and one day after class, Ellen asks you to read some of her poems.

You notice the A on Ken's critique and read: "Your performance demonstrated a keen understanding of the dynamics of the scene. Fine work." You remember he did something from a Shakespeare play, one you didn't know. You heard him tell Jeff that it was a scene he performed for his acting class. You're glad the round is over. Half the time you weren't sure if you were getting the writer's point. You even weren't sure about some of the lines in "The Starry Night," like the one about the moon and its "orange irons." You've always liked to read but never for classes. Teachers can make you feel as if you're too stupid to read a thing. They never assign a Tom Robbins or a Barbara Kingsolver.

As you set up the next round, you're determined that everyone in class will understand how performance is ideological, from the texts we privilege, to the subjects we embrace, to the performances we applaud. You want them to see how performance offers the individual a forum, a space from which to be heard. You want them to recognize how performance is power, a tool for the advocate. You want them to embrace performance as an opportunity, a chance to make their own feelings and beliefs known. Your assignment is simple: "Think of yourself as a political agent who wishes to foreground your own ideology in performance. Combine two or more texts, your own or others', as you mark your rhetorical space." You discuss intertextuality and the potential of holding one text against another. You borrow from Marxism and postcolonialism, without using the labels, to talk about oppression and marginalized voices. You describe several feminist performances as examples, including the one where a woman, puffing on a cigar, parodied male stand-up comics by turning wife jokes into husband jokes. You cringe when Jeff uses his rhetorical space to claim he's oppressed because the "Femi-Nazis" are taking away his rights.

You're not sure what you want to do. You know Jeff's didn't go over well. Jenny's seemed like a God and American pie speech about getting the most out of life. Micha's resistance to becoming a good wife in Japan was interesting. Steven did a powerful performance on censorship. You're scheduled the same day next week as Ellen, who is planning to do some of her poems. You know you can't wait any longer to decide.

You watch Alan take off his Cubs' cap before going onstage. You're pleased not because you have anything against the Cubs but because you've asked Alan to think about his cap as a prop that may or may not work for certain performances. He begins with a direct statement: "I'm gay." His performance is a complex interweaving of the Christian communion ceremony and of lovemaking with his partner. It is a penetrating critique of fundamentalist theology, and it is explicit in its description of gay lovemaking. You are totally engrossed, when Jenny stands up by her seat and says, "Do I have to listen to this?" "No, you are always free to withdraw from any performance you find objectionable," you reply. She exits, and Alan announces he cannot go on. He leaves. You are angry you won't hear the end of the performance. You're disappointed that Alan and Jenny will miss hearing what everyone has to say. You're excited by what is at stake. You're sorry he didn't leave his Cubs' cap on.

You were feeling uncomfortable when Jenny broke in. The class becomes incredibly tense. Then, talk erupts. Steven says he has a lot of gay friends and it's no big deal. Ken breaks in arguing that this performance wasn't just about being gay; it was about being gay as a kind of religion. Ellen counters by noting that it was an attack on those Christians who bash gays. You claim that Jenny was within her rights to leave, explaining that while everyone is free to say what they want, not everyone has to listen. Ken asserts that since Alan listened to Jenny's talk about the power of Christian love, she should have listened to his about gay love. The discussion goes on, and you realize you are missing your next class. Jeff ends the debate thirty minutes into the next hour when he asks if Alan will be graded down for not finishing.

You can always count on Jeff to bring the level of conversation down several notches. But you can measure the richness of a conversation when students forget they are wired to the bell, when they eliminate you as a mediating channel, a refraction point, and when they leave still talking, still questioning, testing with their friends what they wouldn't say in public. You summarize by saying: "Perhaps Jeff's comment best serves to identify an appropriate time for closure. Remember, though, that this is not just about Alan's and Jenny's beliefs. We all must ask: Whose voice would I censor? What principles or beliefs, if any, permit me to silence another?"

That night it becomes clear what you'll do: a performance on racism. You remember that your mother, who has taught in Chicago inner-city schools for years, preaches against racism and still refers to African-Americans as "those people." You interview people about racism, making their comments part of your script. You knew no one would say he or she is a racist, but you show, by quoting from the interviews, how everyone is. You even include some of your own experiences when you acted as a racist. You call your program "A Young White Girl's Reflections about Racism in America."

You're surprised when someone from the campus paper calls to ask you about the class. It seems that Chris interviewed her about racism for her upcoming performance, and she wants to know more about the class for an article she's writing. You answer her questions, choosing your words carefully in the hope that you will not be misquoted. You doubt if her piece will please you. It appears the day before Chris's performance with only minor distortions. You are pleased. That pleasure vanishes, however, when an African-American man, who identifies himself as a member of the Black Alliance Student Organization, arrives to see Chris's performance. After talking with Chris, you let him stay.

You had thought about how the two African-American students in the class, Ellen and Sonya, might respond. Having an outsider witness the performance was a different matter. It was frightening. But you couldn't say no when asked if it was agreeable to you if he stayed. So, you did it, and you did it well. The class raved, including the instructor: "Not only was it scripted with skill and performed with considerable polish, but it was truly insightful, penetrating, and courageous." The comment you will remember though came at the end. The uninvited guest spoke, slowly and solemnly, from the back of the room: "I'm always amused when I watch white guilt."

Last days always carry a note of sadness. You recognize that this group, who has been pulled together and apart by the performative enterprise, will end. To be honest, some of the group you are glad you won't see again. Others you will genuinely miss and will think about over the years. You close class by thanking the group: "I want to thank you for your fine performances over the semester. Many will be with me for a long time. I won't easily forget Marge's performance on sexual abuse, Micha's thoughtful reflections about the role of the Japanese woman, Ellen's presentation of her own deeply moving poems, Alan's personal narrative on being gay, Chris's incredible growth culminating in her performance on racism, and many others. I want to thank you for reminding me through your work that performance matters, that it has consequences. I want to thank you for being alive enough, sensitive enough, caring enough to let performance be meaningful in your lives." You hear their applause.

4
Telling Tales

This is a story about telling tales, how we get them, how we tell them, and how we hear them. We are this story's characters; we are its plot. Our stories narrate our lives; our stories are personal and political. Our tales reach out to others, and they reach over others. They are individual, social, and ideological acts in an ongoing process of construction. They make us as they are made. We are their creators and their creation. Our tales are telling.

Stories of History, Culture, and Identity

I've been collecting them for over forty-three years now. Started when I was a kid. Once I drove all the way to California just to see one. I would have bought it too if this guy (Jenkins was his name) would have given just an inch on the price. I had to add on this room for my collection. I think I did it in '78 or '79. You can see that I'm running out of room again. I never know where the time goes when I come in here. I like to just hold them in my hands. You see that one: I got it back in '62. It still is one of my favorites, but it isn't worth nearly as much as some of the others. This one would bring a pretty price. I heard somebody over in Indiana got over three hundred dollars for one just like this. And this one is special because my kids got together and bought it for me. I had my eye on it for over a year, and one day I noticed it wasn't in the window down at Shelby's anymore. I was real disappointed I hadn't gotten it. Then, my kids surprised me with it on my birthday. My wife says I'm nuts spending so much time and money on this, but I think of it as an investment. Every day it's worth more. The cost goes up and up.

A comedian, whose name I've lost, does a routine about the difficulty he has in picking up "chicks." He says: "I'm considering moving to a Third World country where I think I would be a hit with the babes: 'Yea, I got shoes.'"

I fixed myself a cup of Starbucks and poured her an Absolut. She looked beautiful dressed in her Calvin's and Polo top. I knew this was the real thing. I thought: "Just do it." But before I said a word, she put her Absolut down on my latest copy of *GQ* and whispered, "You deserve a break today." She smiled and then added, "What you want is what you get."

I had to reach out and touch her. "Like a good neighbor, I'm here for you," I said. "With me, you are in good hands."

"Together, we have a piece of the rock," she answered, glancing at her Rolex. "I'm expecting a call coming in on my cellular."

Her policy to do more first attracted me to her. Life's too short not to get all the gusto you can. She smiled at me again—nothing gets remembered like a smile. Oh, what a feeling to know the length she would go to for our pleasure.

"I've come a long way, baby," she said, loosening my Dior tie. "You're my true choice."

"I love," I murmured back, "what you do for me."

"After we're finished," she said, unbuttoning my Ralph Lauren shirt, "all day long people will ask what you're smiling about. You'll love the way we fly."

I shouted with joy, "We are a constant in a violently changing world."

Well, it's no secret, she knows how to ignite the night. Together, we bring good things to life.

You want history. You want my story. You already know it. I was in the camps. I lost my mother and father and my sisters, Rebecca and Ruth. You want more than that. You want me to tell of being raped and being glad I wasn't being sent away. Is that what you want? Well, I won't tell it. Not anymore. I won't. Get your own history.

> "I like these."
>
> "I have to get the lawn seeded."
>
> "I need to buy some more jeans."
>
> "I want to join that club."
>
> "I have to get a massage."
>
> "I want a new car."
>
> "I need a bigger place."
>
> "I crave those."
>
> "I require my time alone."
>
> "I desire you."
>
> "I think I'll have some more."

It was all part of my plan. It's working out just like I thought it would. Chicano is big now. I got my story to sell. I started when I was fourteen.

I've done seventy-three jobs. Wrote them all down in here. This is my history. I'll do my time, but when I'm out, I'll be free. No more worries. The best thing for me was getting shot. That made the story good, made it good for TV.

When you are old, hoard your stories like a miser would gold. If you lose them, you'll have nothing left.

America, I don't know how to write your history. I don't want it told in wars, in presidents, in dollars. I don't want to count those behind bars, those who illegally crossed borders, those who have no homes. I don't want to hear of the hungry, of the sick, of the poor. I don't want to see the battered, raped, abandoned. I don't want to feel the pain of the deceived, debased, destroyed. I don't want to smell the breath of the betrayed, banished, bruised. I don't want to touch it. I don't want it set in monuments, statuary, or memorials. I don't want it stored in museums, archives, repositories. I want another heritage, another history, one that brings light to the eyes of its people, one that lifts weight from the shoulders and from the heart, one that must happen before it can be written. I want a history I can sell with pride.

Stories of Race, Class, and Gender

White (guilty), middle-class (guilty), divorced (guilty) man (guilty) seeks same (guilty) for long-term relationship without guilt.

On the night Dr. Martin Luther King was assassinated, I had gone to the New Orleans Athletic Club for a workout and a massage. When it was time for my rubdown, I got my usual man, Hank. Hank is a big man, strong. He was headed to college on a football scholarship until he ripped up his knee. "Good evening, Hank. How are you tonight?" I said.

"Fine, sir. I'm doin' fine. You just set yourself right down here, sir," Hank answered, sounding not quite himself.

I was ready for Hank's powerful hands to take away the stress from the office. He could work each muscle until you felt like a new man. He began as usual but soon started beating my back to the rhythm of his mumblings:

> "They had no right (whop).
>
> They had no right (whop).
>
> He was a good man (whop).
>
> Dr. Martin Luther King (whop).
>
> He was king (whop)."

His rhythm increased, his blows became harder, his speech clearer. I was, I must admit, getting scared.

"To shoot that man down, (wham), my man down (wham).

It's just not right, (wham), just not right (wham)."

"Hank," I said, "I think that's all I need for tonight."
"But I'm not finished yet, sir," he answered, placing his large hand in the middle of my back to hold me in place.

"No, I'm not (whack) finished yet (whack).

I'm not (whack) finished yet (whack)."

Well, as far as I was concerned, he was finished. The next day I called, explained what happened, and got him fired.

Being middle class in America means:

Most of the people you meet consider themselves middle class.

Most of the people you meet are white.

Most of the people you meet live in three or four bedroom homes.

Most of the people you meet are a part of a two-car family.

Most of the people you meet assume college will follow high school.

Most of the people you meet think that you want the same things out of life as they do.

Most of the people you meet cannot fit all their clothes in their closets.

Most of the people you meet are someone's boss.

Most of the people you meet are heterosexual, publicly.

Most of the people you meet would rather be watching television.

Most of the people you meet take one- to two-week-long summer vacations.

Most of the people you meet have several phones.

Most of the people you meet belong to one or more clubs.

Most of the people you meet believe that you have a more sexually active life than themselves.

Most of the people you meet would rather be with their pets.

Most of the people you meet can name hundreds of movie stars.

Most of the people you meet own exercise equipment they don't use.

Most of the people you meet have several small kitchen appliances.

Most of the people you meet have medical, home, car, and life insurance.

Most of the people you meet celebrate every major holiday.

Most of the people you meet are members in a church.

Most of the people you meet marry more than once.

Most of the people you meet smell of artificial fragrances.

Most of the people you meet carry several major credit cards.

Most of the people you meet vote when it's convenient.

Most of the people you meet are sure they are right.

When I found out I could make more collecting social security than working for them, I quit. They were surprised. I guess they thought I liked getting on that bus every day to go raise their kids and clean their toilets. "Freddie," they said—my name is Fredricca, but they called me Freddie—"How can you leave us? This place just won't be the same without you."

"Well, you'll find another girl," I answered. "I'm getting old. I can't do what I once did." They accepted that as a simple statement from an old woman. But it was more. They'd find another girl like they'd find another vacuum if the old one broke. I was nothing but equipment to them, and they were nothing but a check to me. We all pretended to have, within strict bounds of course, this affection for one another. What I couldn't do was pretend anymore. Twenty-two years is enough. I could still do the work, but I didn't like those people, and they only liked me for what I could do for them. I was their maid, their servant, their nigger.

Those twenty-two years are too hard to forget. I remember what it was like to get those handouts for my children, those toys and clothes soiled with their use. They thought I'd be so grateful to get their trash. I took those things because I was too poor to make any other choice. But I hated myself searching through their garbage. I remember hearing those children I raised calling me "nigger" when I had to correct them and their mother saying they didn't mean any harm by it. Well, harm was done. I never forgot what was always just under the surface. I remember when my child had pneumonia. I had to leave him in order to take care of their child with the sniffles. "Freddie, we need you," they said. They needed me to keep all bother from their lives, to keep their lives dust free. I remember when my husband died and they asked if they would be safe if they came to the funeral.

As I sit here rocking, I guess I remember too much. But I'm going to rock until I can rock away the memories like a momma rocks away a baby's tears. I'm going to rock for all the years I gave them. I'm going to rock for the shame of it all. I'm going to rock until I sleep.

Last night I was preparing for my Performance and Literary Criticism class by reading Kay Capo and Darlene Hantzis's "(En)Gendered (and Endangered) Subjects: Writing, Reading, Performing, and Theorizing Feminist Criticism" article. I was just about to finish the point about language as a site of resistance when Tessa, my nine-year-old daughter, entered the study and dropped one Barbie and two Ken dolls right on top of the page.

"Which one of these Kens would make the best husband for Barbie?" she asked.

"I don't know," I answered, remembering Capo and Hantzis's ideas about agency. "Why don't you let Barbie decide?"

"Oh sure," she quipped back, "like she has a brain and could decide. She's just a Barbie."

Multiple choice question: Which of the following statements about this incident are true?

a. This incident proves that daughters will always seek a father's approval. That is, they have little choice but to yield to the patriarchal symbolic.

b. This incident demonstrates the hegemonic power of cultural institutions, e.g., marriage.

c. This incident suggests that even young female children equate attractiveness with stupidity.

d. This incident illustrates that young girls, perhaps even younger than nine years old, understand something of the complex discursive systems they must negotiate in order to establish their identities.

e. None of the above. It's just a cute little story.

f. All of the above.

His office was separate, a plush thirty by thirty square, filled with all the right touches: a small cherry conference table and matching desk, leather chairs, a wet bar. He supervised five white clerks and ten black drivers for a wholesale grocery company. Each morning before they could make their runs, the drivers had to get clearance from one of the clerks, a system designed to ensure that the grocery orders had been filled and loaded correctly. After the Friday runs, the drivers would line up outside the boss's office for their week's pay, but he wouldn't give out any checks until all the drivers had returned. While they waited, they faced an Old World map that hung on the wall for years. Someone had altered it in blue ink by adding a "g" to "Nigers."

Did the drivers wonder who was responsible for this offense, who could have been such a blatant racist to have added that "g," who in authority, after seeing the alteration, would have left the map on the wall? Did they wonder if they should take some action—rip the map down, explain their objections to the boss, question the clerks—and risk losing their job? Did they wonder if they should tell their wives and children what they confront to get their minimum wage checks? Or did they dream of a place where only a few white blemishes might mar the beauty of a pure black space?

And did the clerks and the boss think this was funny, a joke that all who matter would surely find humorous? Did they think this would not give offense? Did they think that the drivers wouldn't care or be hurt by such a message? Did they think they needed such public reminders to keep the blacks in their place? Did they think they could continue such actions without consequences? Did those whites who thought it should come down, but did nothing, want it down simply out of a fear based in a racist presumption that an angry black is a violent one? And why didn't I, after watching my dad hand out those checks for years, ever say anything?

I'm what they call a "Yat." That means I grew up in a blue-collar neighborhood like the Irish Channel or the Ninth Ward in New Orleans. That means I grew up talking with an accent that sounds closer to Brooklyn than to anything southern. "Yat" comes from the greeting "Where are you at?" The greeting is an inquiry, of course, into another's psychological well-being and requires considerable linguistic gymnastics if one isn't born to it to produce just the right inflection and the proper slurring of syllables. That also means I grew up watching the rich kids, those from old money who lived around St. Charles Avenue and those from new money who lived by the Lake. Neither group had much use for us. I've been away from New Orleans for years now—I went to college, got a good job, learned to talk like a midwesterner—but I'm sure that they would still think of me as a Yat.

Some things sit inside you like a rock. You might be able to chip away at that rock, but it's solid. You don't forget how they would look at you. It was as if you were breathing too much air, their air. You don't forget how they treated your sister. A "charmer" they called her, meaning she was good for only one thing. You don't forget as you walk on your own plush lawn how you were arrested for pissing on the lawn of that house on the Lake. You remember what you were thinking when they grabbed you: "I piss on your lawn, I piss on your bush, and I piss on you. I piss on you for having what I don't and for thinking you're better than me because you do."

Now I have it all—the house, the cars, the money, the perfect speech— and this is what I think: I am better than my friends and family that I left behind, and I hate myself for believing so.

You say that those young boys come from nice families, those boys who drove by and knocked my Jarvis off that overpass with their baseball bat just because of the color of his skin. Well, what is my nice family going to do now? What are we going to do without Jarvis? I ask you that! What are we going to do? So don't you dare tell me about their regrets. I don't want to hear it. I'm not interested in their story.

Stories of Politics, Ideology, and Ethics

Each spring the performance studies faculty members solicit production proposals from our graduate students for the season of the following academic year. The faculty reads the proposals and decides who will have an opportunity to direct. The season usually consists of six shows a year that feature social or political themes. The bias of the theatre is liberal, perhaps radical. Often students will discuss their proposals with the faculty before submitting them. One day I am sitting in my office when a doctoral student asks if she might chat about a possible production for the upcoming season.

"I want to do a show around Christian testimonies, people who have stood up for their Christian beliefs," she says.

I knew that she held strong Christian beliefs. I also knew that this bright, articulate person is a most capable performer and director, the kind of graduate student we want to do a show. I respond: "I am not sure how well that theme would be received by the faculty. Have you considered opening up to other types of testimony, expanding to include others who stand up for what they believe—political activists, courtroom witnesses, whistle blowers? We discuss the possibilities for over an hour. She leaves, and I'm feeling that I could support the proposal if it is enlarged in the way we outlined. The proposal arrives on the deadline: a show on Christian testimonies.

When the faculty get together to make their decisions, there are several more proposals than there are slots. Some proposals will not be accepted. "What do you think about the show on Christian testimonies?" I say.

"Well, I think she has written a fine proposal, and I have complete confidence that she could do this well, but I just don't want this on our stage," a faculty member states. "Besides," another faculty member adds, "there are plenty of opportunities for people to hear that message." We all nod in agreement and move on. The day after we announce the upcoming season, I receive a note:

> Thanks for the time you gave me to discuss my proposal. After I thought about it, I just felt I had to propose the show that I wanted to do. I've also come to realize that despite all the talk around here about privileging all voices, despite all the discussions about opening up dialogue, and despite all the lip service to providing a space for the oppressed, the question really is: Whose voice are you willing to silence and for what reasons?

Favorite excuses and their underlying subtexts:

> "I gave at the office."
> (Don't bother me.)
> "I would help if I had the time."
> (Don't bother me.)
> "I can't afford to give any more."
> (Don't bother me.)
> "That's not my problem."
> (Don't bother me.)
> "They should learn to take care of themselves."
> (Don't bother me.)

"I want to talk with you about how your presentation can be read as homophobic, racist, and sexist," I say, trying to contain my anger. "I know your intent was comic," I continue, "but comedy at the expense of others is never funny. So when you write and perform a script that stereotypes and mocks gay, African-American, and women's behavior, you can't expect anyone except homophobic, racist, or sexist people to appreciate your work."

"You mean," he replies, "that you're going to grade me down just because of some PC stuff?"

"Right."

In a note I wrote to a female colleague, Dr. L., I asked for a favor by using the phrase "Can I twist your arm?" Upon reflection, I realized that the phrase might be objectionable and jotted off a note of apology. She wrote back: "It must be tough being a man." A week later in a general conversation over lunch I mentioned that I thought a particular article was "seminal." Dr. L. remarked, "Given its etymology, are you sure you want to use the word 'seminal'?" In both incidents, I felt, and rightly so, the power of feminist hegemony. I wonder if I'll be graded down.

Border Crossing

1

Going south you see the signs
a faceless family of three
a father, mother and child,
fleeing across the highway
mother clasping the child's wrist
as the father leads the way
"CAUTION" the sign clamors
above the dark family figures
so the California motorists
won't trouble their day by
an accidental road kill

2

Build the fences higher
Arrest them 'til they tire

Call the border patrol
We must keep control

Hire more guards
They're coming in our yards

Shine your lights tonight
We must protect our rights

Build the fences higher

3

Crossing over, you wait
to be examined. Innocent
as skin you slide right through
passing under their poison eyes

4

Look at the line
Tell me what's fair
Look at the line
Then list what's mine

Look at that child
Peeking through the fence

And tell me, por favor,
How a line makes sense

5
Watched by the guards
they pass dollars and pain
at Border park. They can visit
through a chain-linked fence
before it runs into the Pacific
driven solid into the sand
out just far enough to tempt
but too far for success.
It is an engineering feat.

Who is pleased that Robinson's Richard Cory "went home and put a bullet through his head"? Who will celebrate his demise?

Stories of Value and Response

I was in Rosetta News bookstore looking at the new titles in literary criticism when they entered. They went straight to the tattoo magazines, I guess, in the hopes of finding a picture of another tattoo that they would like to add to their bodies. After a while, he looks up and notices the poetry section: "Wow, look. They have a bunch of Bukowski stuff. Should we buy one?" "I told you," she says, "I don't do books."

During my Introduction to Feminist Studies class, Jackson, the only African-American guy in the course, leaned over and was asking me out when the teacher says, "Stop everything. When a person of color speaks, we must all listen."

Select your favorite Jackson response as an ending to the story:

a. How rude! How rude to me and to those who were speaking. As feminists, we should never let our principles trample the individual.

b. By positioning me as a speaker for all blacks, I am oppressed once again, despite your noble intent.

c. I was just asking her out as a gesture toward racial equality. My intent is to blur the bloodlines.

d. Sounds like feminist Honkie b.s. to me.

e. [Write your own].

Stories come in three parts:

"Once there was a farmer who had three daughters. . . ."
"And she was given three wishes. . . ."
"Once there were three little pigs. . . ."

See above.

"Does it matter to you that the poem you performed to the picture of your opposite sex partner is about love between same sex partners?" I ask. I want to know if the student recognizes this fact and if she sees her performance as potentially co-opting.

"Love is love" is all she answers. I want to believe her, to accept that this nineteen-year-old is right. I want to trust her simple truth. But I can't: Some loves cost. My response, though, is to nod in consent, refusing to co-opt her idealism with my old cynicism.

Reading *Vanity Fair*, you see things to buy: Microsoft Windows 98, Guess Knits, Estee Lauder, Clinique, Bombay Gin, Cadillac, St. John Faux Fur, Lancome Rouge Sensation, Evian, Absolut Vodka, Michal's Fine Jewelry, Neiman Marcus, Boss, Victoria's Secret, Stratus Dodge, Calvin Klein, Adrienne Vittadini Bed and Bath Collections, Dakota Smith Eyewear, Giorgio Armani, Elizabeth Taylor's Black Pearls, Chivas Regal Blended Scotch Whisky, London Fog, Gucci, Tiffany's, Waterman, Elizabeth Arden, B&B Cognac Liqueur, Valentino Boutique, Perrier, Swatch, Ralph Lauren, Polo, Coach, Chanel, Lexus, and so on.

Reading *Vanity Fair*, you see people to note: Katharine Hepburn, Susanna Moore, Bill Gates, Anne Rice, Jennifer Larmore, Steven Spielberg, Randy Newman, Wendy Wasserstein, Colin Powell, Alexander Liberman, Denzel Washington, Greg Kinnear, Carol Channing, Rupert Murdoch, Michael Eisner, Carly Simon, Julie Andrews, Oliver Stone, Michael Jackson, Sandra Bullock, Newt Gingrich, Tim Roth, Barbra Streisand, Robert Mapplethorpe, O. J. Simpson, Nicole Kidman, and so on.

Reading *Vanity Fair*, you remember Bunyan's *Pilgrim's Progress*.

The class on Performance and Gender continued beyond the hour and spilled out into the main office. The class had been doing an exercise in which the men were invited to wear breast prosthetics to gain some sense of that bodily experience. Several women in the class were dismayed that some of the men in the class were resistant to the exercise.

"I can't believe that you were unwilling to even try it," one woman complained.

"How would you feel if I asked you to wear a stuffed penis?" a man retorted.

As the debate continued, more and more people joined the fray. Some questioned whether the prostheses could simulate a breasted experience.

Several felt that the prostheses, while surely not perfect, gave some indication of what it might be like to have breasts. People who were not in the class began trying the breasts prostheses on. I, along with several other male faculty members, joined in.

The next day the dean called to make sure that the student who was complaining in his office had not fabricated the entire story. "Surely," he said, "you weren't wearing fake tits?"

I didn't know what to do. I hadn't see anything like it before. But there it was. Right in front of me. I wanted to do something, but I couldn't. I didn't know how, and I was afraid. It was horrible. People shouldn't have to suffer like that.

Telephone Story

Caller 1: Growing up as a young man, I thought all the world was mine for the taking.

Caller 2: As he was growing, he believed everything was his.

Caller 3: Before he grew up, he knew how to get everything he wanted.

Caller 4: Growing up, he learned how to take everything.

Caller 5: Grown, everything he took he ruined.

Caller 6: His whole life is in ruins.

Caller 7: Hey, I heard you've come on some hard times.

Some stories have faulty starts ("come on, spit it out"). Some stories have poor endings ("then what?"). Some stories are too long ("if I knew you were going to tell me how to make a watch, I wouldn't have asked you the time"). Some stories are too short ("is that all?"). Some stories have no plot ("so?"). Some stories are too complicated ("I just don't get it"). Some stories have unlikable characters ("who cares?"). Some stories have too much detail ("get to the point!"). Some stories have too few details ("tell me more!"). Some stories are filled with existential angst ("I just don't think I can go on").

After reading the manuscript, I thought I'd never seen such self-indulgent tripe. But, of course, I couldn't tell him that.

5

A Day's Talk

Good morning, honey.
I'm taking off for the office. See you there.
Bye.

I am not surprised by how little I said to my wife that morning. Actually, I thought I would be leaving before she was awake. Mornings are never a good time for us to talk.

I AM A PRIVATE PERSON. I DON'T LIKE ANYONE KNOWING ANYTHING ABOUT ME THAT I DIDN'T DECIDE TO SHARE MYSELF.

Good morning, J.
How are you doing?
Okay. Okay. Hanging in there. Trying to figure out how to work this VOR. Do you know how this works? It's supposed to be voice activated.
I mean it seems like. . . . It says "On." Okay. Now it's going. Maybe this is it.
But then it should stop after I stop talking. Amazing! And it went. That's how it works.
Yes I do. Yes I do.
I think so. I think the answer is no regardless of what the technicality says she can do. Even if the technicality says you can do this, it would have to be through consent of her committee.
Don't you think?
I don't think there is any . . .
I really do worry about that from a legal point of view.
Yea. As long as she is a student in good standing, I don't know if we have another choice.
I'm sure plenty of people are kicking themselves in the butt for that.

You already see the logic shaping this piece. You assume a cautious stance.

46

A Day's Talk

Sharing my talk may share too much. This is, nevertheless, an accurate record of my day's talk. I have not cut a thing. The only substitution is to exchange first initials for names. Does that say too much?

You wonder if the student recognizes herself in this conversation. You wonder if there is some risk in sharing this kind of talk. You wonder about the ethics of it all.

IF I KNEW THEY WERE TALKING ABOUT ME, I'D SUE.

Hi J. How are you?
Good, thanks.
I just got here just a couple of minutes ago.
So we went ahead and got the new one, uh?
Sure. You bet. Look, I'm all ucky. I'll get it.
Okay.
Okay. Alright J. Ha, ha, ha.
I have my sugar. Thanks J.
Okay.
I will. I will.
It's good.

I DON'T MIND GETTING COFFEE BECAUSE IT ISN'T EXPECTED.
IF IT WERE, WELL, THAT'S ANOTHER MATTER.

The original vision for this piece is different than what you are reading. My intent was to record my day's speech and place it alongside of all the things that my body happened to produce in one day. I called it "A Day's Production." I had photographs of all the things you can imagine.

You thank the Lord for small favors and wonder if any woman should get any man a cup of coffee.

Yea?
Sure.

Hello?
Okay, great.
Hello?
Good morning.
Fine, thanks.
I don't think I have real good news for you. Let me tell you about our four graduate concentrations and what you might be able to do in pub-

lic relations. We have four different areas for graduate study: Rhetoric and Philosophy of Communication, Interpersonal Communication, Communication Education and Instruction, and Performance Studies. So really we don't have a graduate area in public relations.

Okay, bye.

To speak on behalf of the department is nothing more than an act of public relations. To speak on behalf of myself is nothing more than an act of personal relations.

You wonder whether to let him speak on your behalf is nothing more than an act of self-betrayal.

How are ya?
Good.
Good, good, good. Yea. Thanks.
Yea.

Recognizing its banality, you fill in the conversation.

No. They continue tomorrow.
Yes. Yes.
Not until after lunch. So.
It will be interesting to see what they come up with.
How they might just harm themselves in the name of art. Ha, ha. ha.
We shall see. Ha, ha.
I think it is one thing to say I understand the rationale and why they did it. . . .
Oh.
I agree.
Ah. You can build such a wonderful feminist case. How dirt is situated. But, I mean, one of the things I like about it is that it makes me question the taboo.
Yea.
At other times I say, I see what it is covering up and that's wrong.
Yea. It gives me time to reflect about it, and for that, I'm grateful. And I'm grateful too at times that I'm not the one who had to do that. I mean, I much rather ask why I would or would not be comfortable doing that. What is it about my own upbringing that would keep me from doing such a thing?
Despite all my revolutionary talk, despite all my real belief in radical politics, I am a conservative, middle-class, white guy.
But I mean I think it is really true.

There are ways in which I just can't give up some of those privileges. I mean, how can I go play golf at the country club and then preach revolution. I mean, you just can't put those things together. There is no resolving that conflict.

I just don't find the space in my life to practice what I preach.

I can't create that space.

It really is.

Good old white guilt. Ha, ha.

Yea. You always can see it coming.

Yea, me too. Ha, ha.

Some things I'd rather not confess.

<u>Some things you'd rather not witness.</u>

I THINK HE ENJOYS THE CONFESSION. IT'S HOW HE CAN CLAIM PURE INTENTIONS WITHOUT GIVING UP A THING. IT'S A POLITICAL SHAM.

Yea, come on in.

Sure. Sure.

Feels better.

Good.

Yea.

That surprises me. Didn't you include Fine and Speer? "A New Look at Performance"?

I think it's okay.

I did.

It would be really nice if we could get it in everyone's boxes by tomorrow.

Yea.

It's not binding in any way, although we do need to clear it with the committee.

No. Ha, ha, ha.

Okay? Are we set?

Good.

What time on Monday?

Alright. Good.

HE ALWAYS WANTS TO ADD ONE MORE THING. HE ALWAYS WANTS TO TOY WITH YOU.

<u>You are pleased to see that the Fine and Speer piece would be missed from a graduate student's reading list.</u>

I'm just suffering from stupidity.

I'm trying to do T's pages.

I thought it was going to be a close game at the end. But, but neither Pippen nor Jordan could hit a shot. Before the game I predicted that they would win.

Right.

I didn't think that Seattle could do it.

Right. Right.

I would have loved to be in that locker room after the game.

They would just have to feel ashamed.

M's theory is that this is all planned, that they couldn't end it in just four games, that it would be too much of an economic loss, that they needed that extra television revenue.

I can't imagine the talk that would make it happen. How does that talk transpire?

I can't imagine either that the money that they would make from a fifth game would be more than what they would get from all the hype you'd get out of the history and having swept and winning a championship. They're not going to do anything that would put that in jeopardy. Surely, surely not.

Yea.

I don't believe it.

You restored my faith. M had put a crack in it. Ha, ha, ha.

M went upstairs. "If you're going to watch that . . ."

Fun. I watch to the last play, even though I knew the outcome with five minutes to go, or ten minutes to go.

Got to make plans around that.

Does this sound like men's talk, familiar as any cliché, familiar as any old stereotype?

<u>You understand that men's talk is safe talk, until you look underneath, until you see what is being held in place, until you become the subject.</u>

That looks like ours.

Sure.

Finish up. Send it to her.

Sure.

I FELT DISMISSED.

Do you know how long that process might be?

Great. Alright.

Good. Good. Good.
Did I also hear the bad news that there is only two rather than four?
Heck.
Make you nervous?
Did you realize it was missing?

<u>You know what is going on in this piece. You are beginning to believe
that too much is missing. You are beginning to grow impatient, but you
push on.</u>

Did you talk to her?
I need to get her out of bed. Right?
Don't you think?
Hello, sweetheart.
You're not out of bed yet? How could that be?
Oh. You're tired. Well, you know what time it is?
It's eleven o'clock.
Oh. Okay. Cause your mom is planning to take you to lunch. Okay?
Don't go back to sleep on us now.
Alright sweetie. Love ya.
Bye-bye.

*More talk that fits another stereotype? It is the typical father-daughter
interaction, where she is the thirteen-year-old princess and I am the insufferable pea.*

How are you?
Sure.
Me too. Me too.
Okay.

Hi, N. How are you?
Good.
I have no idea.
Check with J. Put the bug in his ear.
Well, we'll see today. We'll see what happens.
Alright, good. Are you getting excited?
I mean, does it sound exciting?
Great.

So you don't have to worry about that?
Okay.

You cannot decide just how irritated you are. Perhaps you are amused.

Hello.
Thanks.
Hi, darling.
Outing at three. No, I can't make it. Thanks for the message though, sweetie.
Okay sweetie. Bye-bye.

Isn't that sweet? What more could an insufferable pea ask?

I WANTED HIM TO DEDICATE THIS BOOK TO ME, BUT HE WOULDN'T DO IT.

There's nothing there that I need.
Okay. Good.

Hello.
Thanks.
Hi, L.
Fine. How about you?
Six months. Maybe eight. That is a long time to make you wait.
Yea.
I've got one out that is over a year now. The process is just awfully slow. It's really infuriating.
Depending.
Plan to work. That's my big plans. I plan to do some of my work instead of graduate advising and all of that kind of stuff.
Yea.
Okay. Okay. I just finished one chapter, and I'm doing the very last one now. So that's where I am.
Yea. I'm excited. At least I'm going to call it ready to go out.
Of course, one never knows. You know.
Then you just sit and wait.
That sounds interesting, L. That might work really nicely.
Alright.
Okay. Good.
Okay. Talk to you soon.
Bye.

The difference between a student and a colleague is that a colleague will ask about your latest project. Students, rightly so, only want to talk about their own work. Most of the time, it is easier to talk with students.

A Day's Talk

<u>You remember times when you asked colleagues about their work, waiting for your turn to talk about your own.</u>

Is it just you and me?
Then this isn't one of the new ones then.
This very moment. I'm taping.
That's true. That's true.
Yes.
I am. I am. It doesn't matter.
Yes.
They think I'm a fool. They know I'm a fool. Ha, ha, ha. I been discovered. Ha, ha, ha.
Quatro's?
Quatro's?
Are you driving?
I'm right over there.
Yea. I'll drive.
That sounds good.
Ha, ha, ha.
To dream. It's going to happen. He's going to get another job. That's my bet.
No.
At another university.
Yea.
I'd be surprised if he couldn't find another position.
I think so.
I would like to know. I've heard two conflicting stories. One is that he had another episode with his heart. That suggests that it was his doing, his deciding. And the other little scenario is that this was coming, that this was S's move, that this was a gracious way for him to get out. I really don't know which one of those is true.
Yea.
If it is S pushing him out, then B's days are numbered too.
Yea.
They are a team. If you decide one has to go, so does the other.
These are new lines that he wants.
Probably could have taken care of the COLA problems.
Right.
We need a new line to see who we need to fire.
No.
Thanks. We'll use your quarter.
The combination. Pepperoni, thousand island, and diet coke.
Are you traveling?

53

No.
Go back and change her grade. Ha, ha, ha.
That's the only way.
I wonder what the cost is?
This is the one luxury I've given myself. Not to do these anymore. They were always the same, for years, and years, and years. And I just got tired of looking at them. You know?
I mean, the one that always drove me crazy is the one that I'd be graded down on: "Graded Fairly."
Yea. That was always my lowest category, and I know I'm one of the easiest graders in the department.
Yea.
Probably.
So.
Yea, I do. Yea.
There you go.
Thousand. Thanks.
I think of them the same way I think of GRE's—real high or real low probably tell you something.
That middle range just doesn't tell you anything.
You see some pretty low ones, don't you?
I mean, some of our graduate students . . .
Really?
You don't get any real low . . .
Uh uh.
Have any of you gotten straight fives?
I never did.
Yea.
I've seen M get straight fives.
Yea. It made me mad. Ha, ha, ha.
No, you're not.
Just give them all A's.
I play golf with this guy who carries a phone, so we'll be out there on the green and all of a sudden the phone will ring.
It's really very funny to listen to this conversation because invariably it's his wife complaining about the kids.
"Alright, put him on. I'll tell him to stop doing that." Ha, ha, ha.
Me either.
I sure . . .
I sure wouldn't carry it out on the golf course with me.
Yea.
Two more days.
Thanks.

Do you like that piece?
Yep.
Is everyone ready?
Okay.
Fine, thanks.
I was happy because now we get another game.
Here we are.
It's locked.
Sure.
Yea.

Lunch with a crowd, lunch with my colleagues: Do I say too much? Do I say too little? Do I dominate, come off too strong, appear arrogant? Do I fall into the background, a mere blob filling space? Do I ever say anything that's true? Do I say things I wish others would not hear? Do I need to look over my shoulder?

You wonder if there is a reason why you should care. You are irritated.

RON IS JUST RON. NOTHING MORE. NOTHING LESS.

Yea.
Yea.
She is in your office.
She just opened it up.
Yea.

You need the key?
Here it is.
I'll get it later.

I am. This very second.
Yes it is.
Actually this is for a project I'm working on.
This isn't research. This is art. Ha, ha, ha.
Okay.
But they are not community members.
Okay.

Sure.

Sometimes I can be so eloquent.

<u>But most of the time, you can't.</u>

Yes.

Sometimes you can see the signs, but in those cases we try not to call those people.

And, I mean, there were some signs on his. Yea.

We've done it. We'll probably regret it for the next three or four years. Ha, ha, ha.

As I transcribe, I cringe hearing myself laugh.

<u>You try to imagine the laugh. You hear it quite well.</u>

Sure. Sure.

I might get a grade sheet then.

Yea.

And that was C.

Yea.

You don't see any need to act on this, do you?

Good.

I've never heard anyone mention it.

I would think that he would.

What else could one say? I want to hire someone who will get out of my way. Ha, ha.

Yea.

Me either.

The soonest I had it was three years down the line. One can only hope. They are okay.

The best thing that could happen is if they got fired.

It just makes you cringe.

Yea.

Are you hearing a lot of flack about S's request for three lines?

Three new lines for his office?

I don't know if they'll give it to them or not.

I imagine. They've given him everything else.

Yea.

But, I mean . . .

One of the positions is to look at entrenchment. The irony is just a little bit too much. Ha, ha, ha.

It just can't be. They just can't do that.

Just add up the cost of those lines.

That would take care of a lot of problems.

What do I want—three new people in his office or . . . ?

Right.

They're going to win by twenty-five. They are going to kill them. I really think.

In the paper this morning somebody asked him if he was mad, and he said, "Yea." "Does that mean a forty-five point game?" And he answered, "Why stop there?" Ha, ha. ha.

Okay.

I THOUGHT I HAD YOUR SUPPORT.

Could one determine the average number of conversations about Michael Jordan following a game? How often is Pippen, Kukoc, or Rodman the second sentence?

If he is around, he would be across the hall in the graduate student bull pen.

Across the hall, across the landing. The first door you come to on your left.

Sure.

NO ONE ELSE WAS AROUND, SO I ASKED HIM. HE WAS NICE. HE REALLY WAS.

May all questions be so easily answered.

Some interesting stuff.

All five were worth seeing.

Yea.

One that I think you would really appreciate was marvelously elegant in its simplicity. It really moved me. This was L's.

Her graduate career.

The piece starts with her surrounded by academic books. She picks up a book and begins to read. Then she takes out a container of birth control pills and takes one. Near by is a baby doll attached to a string. After she takes a pill, she pulls the string, and the baby moves across the stage further from her. She repeats reading a book for a moment, taking a pill, and then pulling the string. She does this about a dozen times, each time the baby get further away. The piece ends when the baby goes under the curtain.

Each time she pulled the string differently—sometimes with great care, sometimes indifferently.

It was wonderful.

Yea.

Oh, hi.

I was telling E about some of the pieces from class.

Another one I liked a lot was K's. K really participates in a whole body of other artistic enterprises that are very similar. But what we do is we go into the theatre, and he is suspended, swinging above a white canvas. He's got these squeeze bottles with paint, and he's written on the bottom of the canvas, "Push to write." So we start pushing him, and we're wondering if we're going to make him so sick that he'll throw up. He's got tape over his mouth, so we're afraid that he'll asphyxiate himself. But it's really quite fun.

One of the things that is important is that he can't quite get to the edges of the canvas. And so he grunts—umm, umm, umm—until we sense where he wants to go. Finally, he pulls up the edges and wraps himself in the canvas until he has this black paint all over him.

It is really nice. Ha, ha, ha.

It's really funny.

D's was very, very interesting too. She gives this very familiar, very predictable critique except that there are a couple twists in this. We see her putting on makeup, getting ready. She has this Muppet song that has the line about getting ready for a show that says, "It's like a kind of torture." She plays this line over and over, like it's stuck. And then has this other song that has the line "You're too beautiful to be true."

Yea. Exactly.

So then she is trapped.

Yea, in this double bind.

She starts stripping off her makeup, tearing off her clothes. Then, then, and the reaction that this gets is just quite wonderful—just audible gasps—she grabs a clump of hair and cuts it off.

It was really nice and the two musical pieces, I mean, the whole thing of women and their makeup is familiar, but I think those two songs plus the extreme violence of ripping off her clothes and cutting her hair is what makes it.

Yea.

It's fun stuff.

Oh, I love it.

Yea. See you later.

I'M PLEASED TO HAVE MY PERFORMANCE PRAISED. I WOULD, HOWEVER, DESCRIBE WHAT I DID SOMEWHAT DIFFERENTLY.

I wonder if at times performance art works best as conceptual art—complete in the telling.

HE SHOULD HAVE ASKED ME IF HE WANTED TO INCLUDE A
DESCRIPTION OF MY PERFORMANCE.

Despite your irritation, you find yourself interested in the performances.
You wish you had actually seen them.

    Oh, they are?
That would be terrific.
I'm perfectly happy with that.
    I was sure I was going to get it done this afternoon, but I got inter-
rupted so much. Sorry.
    I've everything except your last section. I'm sure I can have it by to-
morrow. Okay?
    See you tomorrow.

I WANT MY PAGES.

There is never enough time. There are always too many pages.

You recognize the truth in what you just read.

    What?
No.
Ha, ha, ha.
Okay.
    I think it's real good. One of the things that is taking me some time is
that I'm doing some close editorial work.
    So, these pages are going to look worse to you.
    Yea, but I think the first section, all the way through the content analy-
sis stuff, is ready to go.
    So your task now is a typing one.
Typing.
Yea, yea. Just put in the changes I've indicated.
Yea.
Yea. Yea.
Uh uh.
I changed your categories a little bit.
Okay. You're welcome to take this if you need it.
I just thought that was a little bit easier.
Right.
I'm pretty sure that's right.
Yea, do the gender thing. Add this in there.
Yea.

Well, I think it works.

What's the criteria?

Good.

You might just make a decision. Either can work.

But it's not in there. If you want to go there, you'll have to add that in.

Oh.

I see.

There is this triad—right? So now I'm back here? The three aesthetic properties of theatre?

But I had no reference for that. Do you see where I was getting confused? I didn't know where in the hell this "five" was coming from.

That's easy to fix. Okay?

Do you really have to get into that at all?

Just . . .

You could just say that Boal writes about blah, blah, and blah, but what is of particular interest here are his notions of . . .

This is driving you crazy. I'm not sure it is worth it.

Just move back and forth between the model and the literature.

Initially, I tried to fix it but . . . Look. Just say that in this particular study I will be evoking Boal's scheme in order to . . .

Remember what you are trying to do here. This is going to be a scheme that you're planning to use in chapter 4. As I think about it, Boal's scheme has to be recovered in the closure of this section.

Yea.

Do I have these?

Good.

I think you can wait on that.

Yea.

I think so.

You can indicate that in the closing paragraph.

If I were you, I sure would.

Sure.

That label is what?

Is that a theme? Is that a finding?

Okay. Talk to me.

Okay.

Does that let you organize what you want to say?

Okay.

You surely can answer it in terms of . . . Well, what you have discovered is that there is no here, no closure that you can point to.

Uh uh.

That seems right.

Yea. Sure. Sure.

You're not going to say that though.
You don't really believe that.
You can do this. I don't think that once you get into it that you're going to have much trouble.
Keep plugging.
Maybe. Maybe, if I get it together.
So anyway. Alright. Uh uh.

I THOUGHT IT WAS CLEAR. I THOUGHT IT WORKED. I THOUGHT I HAD IT.

Is that M?
How are you doing?
That's good.
Alright.
These look good.
People.
"Mastery of"?
"Big old" probably won't work. Ha, ha, ha.
What am I looking for at this point?
And you did it?
Okay. So now I'm to read to see if anything else needs to be done before we go to committee.
That's what we're doing?
Okay. Good.
I think you have a "mastery" of this. Ha, ha, ha.
Right.
Lost in Yonkers has to be available.
Amazing.
In addition, at the end of this . . .
Oh. I get it now.
Hello.
Yes it is.
Okay.
Well, if you called either M or me, you're calling the wrong person.
Who has the completed list is E or J.
They have the complete list if that is what you're looking for.
Okay. Sure will.
Between performances of a show?
I don't want that repeated. That's what I'm trying to get rid of.
This is an "if/then." You always need one to separate those two clauses.
That's profound. Ha, ha, ha.
What does that mean?

Uh uh.

What's real different is that you want to take their narrative concepts that describe life phenomena and apply it to a life phenomenon. It would be awkward and odd to take categories that describe research for your purposes.

Yea.

Right.

Even if you do, where are you going to publish it?

Yea.

That's a question the committee often asks.

TPQ?

Okay.

Yea. I think you'll have to narrow it down.

That should work.

Alright.

Alright with me.

Is everything set?

Good.

See ya. If you have any questions, let me know.

I'M EMBARRASSED TO BE TOLD SUCH THINGS.

I would like to believe that such talk matters, that it makes a difference, that they see it as helpful. I fear giving bad advice, being too easy or too hard, being in the way. I fear the position.

You see only the privilege of holding such a position. You see the insecurity of a fool. You see through your own desire.

J, I'm out of here.

I'll be in early tomorrow.

You have a good night.

Okay.

See ya.

Hello.

Hello. I'm in here.

Yes.

In the living room.

Oh, great! Those look terrific.

You did?

Did you find your light?

Cool.

Pleased with yourself for having stayed with the piece this far, you give yourself permission to skim.

You're home.
I thought so.
They didn't get lost this time.
Okay.
Isn't his birthday on the calendar?
Oh good.
Oh.
It's one of those things you don't know what to do with it.
Oh, my, my, my.
That's your job.
Yes, I am.
I reserve the right to cut what I want.
I reserve the right to cut what I want. Ha, ha, ha.
I got the pictures back.
Sometimes that works and sometimes it doesn't.
I think the battery is wearing down a little bit.
You want to see the photographs?
Where?
Okay.
Hi, K.
How are you?
Good.
Let's take them in here so we can spread them out.
What is it?
Yea.
Some of them I think are real good. Some I don't think work.
I think so.
I like some from the last batch better than these.
It's not clear what that is.
It's actually a kleenex.
This is called "A Day's Hair." That one is called "A Day's Clippings," and so on.
I'm trying to keep them together.
Now, here.
Yea.
These go in there.
That came out alright. Ha, ha, ha.
Uh uh.
That came out real clear.
Part of my question is if these are good enough to put in the book.

No.
Yea, they're essential to the piece.
I guess so.
The name of the piece is "A Day's Production." These photos, they are all named—"A Day's Clippings," "A Day's Hair," you know.
They have to surround the transcript of "A Day's Talk."
The power of the piece is in their association.
Yea.
Anyway.
Once this is done, I'm finished.
Yea.

A dear friend who read this book when it contained the chapter "A Day's Production" wrote a caring note to me in bold print: "EXPUNGE THIS CHAPTER FROM YOUR BOOK."

WISE ADVICE.

I heard from P. She claims she's working.
Yea.
Me too.
She going to Arizona. She says she'll be able to keep writing.
No. No.
I'm skeptical.
That is always hard.
M told me yesterday that she's decided that she doesn't want to stay for her fourth year. She wants to be with her man.
She hasn't decided on her topic yet.
I told her not if she wanted to finish.
She may pull a R.
Lighted.
Yea.
He was terrific.
I think I'll be able to trust her to do things I wouldn't ask others to do.
Yea.
The black widow? Ha, ha, ha.
I don't know if anyone will be using her. Ha, ha.
Yea, that's true.
Sweet, don't you think?
Uh uh.
Those are too small.
It would be different if he was doing a lot of work.
He gives nothing.

Yea.
It's good he's got C.
What are you doing Ruby?
Sweet kitty.
Both are sweet.
Don't eat our candy!
Are you trying to eat our candy?
Okay.

I did not feel the need to reduce Ruby's name to a first initial. Juice is our other cat. I wonder if Ruby would mind if you knew that she likes candy. Juice does not like candy. I am sure he would not mind if you knew that he likes to chew the ends of Tootsie Roll Pop sticks.

<u>You are still waiting for that chewy center, for something rich, for something to sink your teeth into.</u>

MEOW.

Good.
I met with A and M.
That killed most of the afternoon.
I spent some time talking to E about the performance art class.
Do you need help?
Okay.

How much of our talk is talk about talk? How much of our talk is nothing more than a justification of our talk? How much of our justifying talk really justifies?

CAN YOU JUSTIFY MY PRESENCE IN THESE PAGES?

That's how he spends his life.
Yea. You're right. He has real expertise.
Uh uh.
That's all?
Why doesn't he go into business or something?
Really?
J closed the door today all worried about him.
She just didn't like the way she was hearing him talk.
That's my sense.
Yep.
Ha, ha, ha.

I don't know how they negotiate that.
She's working.
In his office?
I've seen her in the main office.
Yea.
Those are two good people.
Yea.
I hope not.

I AM GLAD THAT I AM NOT RECOGNIZABLE, THAT I WILL
REMAIN UNKNOWN.

Right.
T.
T. T. T.
Ha, ha, ha.
T is the most beautiful kid in the whole wide world.
Well, hello. Another beautiful young woman is here. Her name is K.
Oh, I've had great fun taping today.
Probably not.
Because it's too self-conscious.
All day.
You want me to say that you're beautiful?
No?
What would you like me to say about you?
My daughter is a sweet human being who really wants to go to Girl
Scout Camp right now.
Yes.
Just part of it.
Maybe.
Bye-bye.

I LOVE READING ABOUT ME. I LOVE KNOWING I'M IN THESE
PAGES.

I wonder how time will color, change, or cheat her honest claim.

<u>You wonder how he could assume it was her honest claim.</u>

I am. Need any help?
It works.
You want me to check?

Miss K, Miss T, you need to check with K's parents to see if K is go-
ing to join us for dinner.
Macaroni and cheese and hot dogs.
And baked beans and corn.
Because.
Because you have to walk around like this all the time.
So? Who wants to walk around like this all the time?
You do?
What's this? It's disgusting.
No, it doesn't.
Ha, ha, ha.
Okay, great.
Put on another dog. K is joining us.
Why don't you get knives and forks for your mom?
I'll get it.
Drinks?
Diet?
7Up?
You have some English in you?
Would you pass a big cheese please?
Not to mention the big cheese.
The attack of the killer fork?
I don't know why I have the name Mr. Beans.
Uh uh.
Whose going to do the bean song?
The magical fruit?
Uck.
Not I.
Really?
That's true.
I promise you K that there is nothing that you'll say that I'll use.
This is a very good dinner.
Yea, with my mouth full.
Yes. You've done a number of things.
The Barney song.
No.
Ha, ha, ha.
Mean.
It's the big cheese.
It's the big cheese. That's what we keep saying.
That's the idea.
A couple of slices.

Who wants to eat the big cheese?
T wanted to eat the big cheese.
Ha, ha.
I didn't know that about you, K.
Ha, ha, ha.
Not that I recall, darling.
Yea, a couple of times.
I went with others.
You liked it, didn't you?
Ha, ha, ha.
Ha, ha, ha.
I was hoping that she'd turn into an Indian man.
Ha, ha, ha.
It's not "mummmmm." It's "Ommmm." Ha, ha.
We do?
Would you like some cake that T and I made?
It is.
You and I.
Yea.
She has happy faces all over her.
I'm going to bite your head off.
What did she say?
A dumb ass?
There. Take that.
T, your head is all wet.
No you can't.
Where does she get it from?
Look what your mother has done.
You've been productive.
But have you secured lodging?
That's what I would call holding one's personal water.
On our trip back from New Orleans, she never stopped. She never, never stopped. It was like somebody pulled her chain and we couldn't find her off button.
Maybe there were two kinds of mechanisms.
I won't. Ha, ha, ha.
Okay. It's a mixed metaphor.
Who made the rule against mixed metaphors, anyway?
From scratch.
A can.
What is wrong with him?
That's a good reason.
Two weeks.

Ha, ha, ha.
I have to do my dishes.
Clear your plates.
Thanks.

Audiences matter. K, who joins us for dinner, and you who read these pages matter. Speech is always in search of an audience.

IT DOESN'T MATTER TO ME.

<u>As you near the end, you consider what is at stake.</u>

I'm going up to do some work.
Okay.

You're ready to turn in?
Okay, sweetheart.
Good night.
I'll come check on you before I turn in.
Yea. I want my good-night kiss.

Are you about ready to call it a night?
I am. Give me my kiss.
Yea. I think I got what I need.
I love you, darling.
Sleep tight.

I'VE TOLD YOU, I'M A PRIVATE PERSON.

Talk is cheap unless it is about those you love, those who matter in your life, those who care about you. Talk is cheap except when yours is available to everyone, when you can't take anything back, when you don't like how you sound. Talk is cheap if you can walk away from it, put it down, shut it up. Talk is cheap as the day is long.

<u>Talk is cheap unless it happens to waste your time. You could be talking.</u>

On Writing
and Performing

6

The Poet and Performer
Take Stage

The Poem

Homeless Vietnam Vet Crushed
in Back of Garbage Truck

I just happened to glance
in the back of the truck
when I caught sight
It was his foot I saw first
but, by then, it was too late
I almost made my next run
before I packed her but
she rides best when squooshed
If I had waited, he'd still be alive
as any of those deadbeats who
put themselves where they shouldn't
You'd think they would only get in
the empty ones to sleep
I mean with the smell and all
I can hardly stand it myself
when I'm driving and the air
is pushing through up front
I've seen a lot of shit, even
a damn cow once, all decayed
Some other guys have found bodies
but they were already dead
and we've all got our share of
cats—you can hear them screech—
but that's different. I mean

I didn't want to kill nobody
The dumb fuck was just trying
to sleep. I guess he can now.
That foot was sticking out.

The Poet and Performer Meet

The poem is written. I face it as its father, its performer. Its story appeared first as a newspaper account, a report of just the facts. Its life exists beside me; its life exists around me. I stand as its inept god, unable to control it, unable to let it go, unable to know its truth. When I think it is mine, it escapes. It wants another word, a different sound, a new twist. It will not keep still.

The poet offers a gift: I ask only that it be appreciated—if not appreciated, at least given its due attention. Let all the words be read, not skimmed. Let all the sounds be heard, not swallowed. Let the poem approach, slowly, let it come to you. Listen, it is trying to speak. It wants to be taken in. It want to influence. It wants you.

The performer accepts: I take the offering but refuse to be its slave. I will listen and offer words of respect. But I will speak in my own tongue, use those words for my own ends, make something new. Do not expect total allegiance, unquestioning commitment, or steadfast loyalty. Such devotion is a fool's companion, an artist's folly. The empty stage waits, ready for the performer's entrance. One must earn applause.

The Poet and Performer Read the Poem Together

The poet and performer start with a simple question: Where does sympathy lie? The question is driven by a desire to understand. The answer cues attitude, establishes the relationship to the audience, serves as a beginning point. But there is no one answer.

The poem is a plea, a cry for compassion. The speaker, a driver of garbage, wants to forget the foot that was "sticking out." His appeal is based in intent: He had no wish to kill anyone. It was an unfortunate accident. It wasn't his fault. That Vet shouldn't have been there. He needed to pack the truck to make for a smooth ride. Others have made similar mistakes. Now, the Vet can sleep but he can't. He keeps seeing the foot.

The poem is a grotesque comedy, an absurdist play. A bizarre world unfolds, one where a Vietnam Vet sleeps with a decayed cow, where cats screech in their demise, where a foot hangs from a garbage truck. The "dumb fuck" invites our mocking laughter; the pathetic driver calls for our ridicule.

The poem is an indictment, a case based in negligence. It tells of how we have turned our Vietnam Vets into garbage. They are among the dead, a decayed dead cow, dead cats, unnamed dead bodies. They exist among those things that may be listed as "shit." At best, they are an inconvenience, a troubling sight, something to be done with.

The poem is . . . It refuses closure. It wants readers ready to read, ready to put themselves forth, ready to muscle their way in. It waits for the old one-two, a quick skim followed by a right flip of the page. It will take a fall just for them. It has no backbone, no guts, no heart. It is a patsy, an easy mark.

It demands closure. It won't give in; it insists on standing strong. These words flex. They're mean. They mean business. Don't try to bully them; they'll resist, fight back, counter. Go ahead, dance, duck, weave. No points if you don't hit the target.

The Performer Talks to the Poet

The performer's empathic move to the poet ends in the somatic. The body learns its desire. It lives in and for the sensuous. It comes to understanding by feel. Its knowledge is felt. It holds its secrets in its muscles, in its step, in its reach. It finds its truth in the tightened fist, the swift turn, the hesitant tone. It breathes down the poet's neck.

I start rehearsal with the first two lines reading "I just happened to glance / in the rearview mirror." I quickly discover, however, that the physics won't work. I try sitting in front looking in the mirror, but I can't see how the foot could be hanging out so that one could see it from the driver's seat. I change the line to read "I just happen to glance / in the back of the truck." The ambiguity of location allows the physics to rest. I delight when recognizing the associative rhyme: In the "back" of the "truck" the speaker found the "dumb fuck." There is nothing to do with this in performance but say the words. To stress them would be just too much, too much for the realistic illusion.

I try voicing "he'd still be alive / like any of those deadbeats." Through utterance, I learn that "like" must be changed to "as." A simple correction but one I can't imagine I missed before. How could I not see that "like" not only didn't carry the assonance of "as" but disrupted the rhythm of the line? I found it only in performance when I felt that it just took too long to say the line. It wouldn't move with the speed it needed.

Some lines gain flesh in their utterance. "That foot was sticking out" is now vivid, real. I see it in detail, in living color, in horror. I approach it in fascination and repulsion. I hold it steady before me, examining its parts and reacting to its sight. It is tangible as death.

The performer's body also recognizes its reception. It knows that there is meaning in their bodies. When their heads turn away or look down, it knows. When their bodies move from side to side or wobble in their chairs, it knows. When their eyes look with a steady gaze or an empty glare, it knows. And it knows too when their bodies edge forward, suspended by talk, silent and possessed.

The performer's body, then, reminds the head what it forgot. The body remembers by rote, by habits of enactment. It rehearses new understandings. Listen to me, my poet friend, to discover your own writing. When I stumble as I read your lines, the fault may be yours. When I say your poem in surprising ways, you may wish to write again. When I show you things you hardly remember, you may want to start over.

The Poet Talks to the Performer

The poem is more than you can utter. It exists beyond any rendering. It speaks in multiple voices, ready for multiple readers. It will not be contained, reduced to a simple logic or emotion. It always wants more, wants to be taken more seriously, with more pleasure, passion, poignancy. It is always ready to mold you, ready to grab hold, ready to possess you. Your best efforts only invite a return to the poem, an opportunity to question adequacy. You will never measure up; you are your own thing. You may use it, but never master it. You may want it, but never control it. You may hold it (as one might hold a sparrow), but only for a moment. When you do, feel it flutter. It lives its own life.

Notice the last line. That foot will trip you. It contains possibilities you cannot see and, even if you could, you could not translate into performance. The poem is always more than can be said. It finds its power in the ineffable, in the space between words.

The Performer Performs: An Open Rehearsal

The page blurs again. The words squiggle in my nervousness. Some are looking away, some not. I can't enact lesson one: Think about what you're saying. I'm more with them, viewing myself. The garbage truck driver is incidental, the homeless Vet who was killed forgotten. It is just me and them looking at me.

It only kicks in when framed as performance. It only kicks in when I feel something is at stake. It only kicks in when the gaze places me onstage.

The blurred words change position as I speak. They are not in order. Some words are added; others dropped. The need to fill dead space drives the words, drives the rhythm, drives the nerves.

The speaker in the poem is known to me, better than as given. He is without formal education, but not dumb. He is southern, and the politics of that claim haunt me. He is an apologist to others and to himself.

76

He feels the death. He relives it; he will never forget. With time he will elaborate his story.

With time, I will forget. It is a momentary discomfort in a series of such events. I know these moments as performer—the rhythm is wrong in this line, the pause too short here, the planned rate lost. I know them as author—that word mattered, the line breaks are intentional. I know them as teacher—what kind of example are you? I know them as an apprehensive man—the public embarrassment continues.

Somewhere my body knows its place—except, of course, when it moves in performance. My eyes move from the page (he wouldn't be looking at a script) to them (when would he stare at his audience? when would he look away?) to the page (my god, where am I?). My hand moves in gestural support but seems to flap like a dying pigeon. It is not a part of me. I wish to stop and examine it, its strangeness, its world.

And the foot sticks out. I return to the dead. I have seen that foot, fascinated by the physics of it all: booted, bloodied, smashed between iron. And I care more about the living than the dead—his seeing the foot, over and over, a real-life Fellini for us all. Death serves us well.

There are voices here—who shall take stage and at what cost? The players are many—the lookers, the Vet, the driver, myself. Who has the leading role? Who are the bit players? Who is accountable to whom?

Apprehension takes stage by force and leaves only victims.

The Poet Reconsiders

I was a fool to let this poem out of my hands, a fool to believe it had merit. It is nothing but a cheap narrative trick asking for emotions it has not earned. It tries to cash in too easily on cultural wounds: Evoke a Vet and call on the poor if you want a tear. It's yours for the asking.

The poem leaves no room for the reader to maneuver. You can talk of multiple interpretations, but in the end, the poem insists upon how you must feel. It is emotional blackmail daring you to admit you don't care.

As a poet, I am a second-rate tyrant not skilled enough to claim authority but brutal enough to try to oppress. "Let me lead" is a pathetic cry from the incompetent.

The Poet and Performer Talk Again

Most poets believe they read poems better than actors. Most actors disagree. They base their beliefs in understandings of what is best to feature, sound or character. Poets know how words collide, how they wrap around one another, how they sip hot tea. Performers know how people speak, how poems live in attitude, how emotions matter. Poets read with an eye on the page; performers read with an eye on the audience.

Performing for Real

Waiting my turn, I try to listen to the others who perform before me. As I mark time, I catch a phrase here and an image there. I surreptitiously examine the room: Some people I know; some are strangers. It is a good house. I imagine my approach to the stage, avoiding tripping over feet and on stairs. I see myself getting ready, fixing pages and making eye contact before the first utterance. I envision myself in control, confidant as a general commanding troops. I'll be a good little soldier marching to my rehearsal plan. I've gone over it and over it. I know what to do.

The time arrives. I take stage, nervousness surprisingly in check. I begin to speak. I'm doing what I planned. Rehearsal is paying off. I watch them watching me unafraid. I speak from within the poem, from the stance of the persona, from the feelings that count. I know they are listening, understanding, caring. I gain strength as I continue, knowing it's working, knowing I've done what I could, knowing the pieces are in place. It is a delicate act, balanced on a prayer. I drink in celebration from the chalice of my own making. When it is over, I sit, flushed, exhaling the moment. I nod my thanks, wanting both to enjoy and to escape the applause.

Writing for Real

When to let go, to say it's finished, complete? The poem will not rest. It always wants more. One writes as long as one has faith, as long as one believes in its promise. In the end, one simply abandons it. Left on its own, it waits for others. Some treat it with respect; others don't. The poet's job is to pretend he/she doesn't care.

The Performer and Poet Depart

I will take you with me. I have learned from being in your presence. I leave behind words on a page, marks of an encounter. I leave you as a lover might separate from another, changed, wiser, and scarred.

7

Confessions of an Apprehensive Performer

Prologue

To begin. To act. It is always a chance. A chance to win, a chance to lose. They will be looking; it's their job. Audiences come to see what is put before them. They judge. There is no escape, except the back door. Stand up. They are always there, looking, waiting. Talk is cheap, unless it's yours.

Scene 1: Getting Started

Voice 1: I can do it. I'm standing here.

Voice 2: They're watching. You're fixing your clothes! Fixing clothes is just a nervous habit.

Voice 1: Alright, I've stopped.

Voice 2: So what are you going to do now?

Voice 1: Begin.

Voice 2: Well, go ahead.

Voice 1: But they're looking.

Voice 2: Of course they're looking. Did you expect them to come with bags over their heads?

Voice 1: No.

Voice 2: Well, get started.

Voice 1: Okay, okay. Let me fix my notes.

Voice 2: You'll probably think you lost a page.

Voice 1: Did I?

Voice 2: No, but you really need to begin.

Voice 1: Let me take a deep breath. Then I'll start.

Voice 2: We're waiting.

Voice 1: "Ladies and gentlemen . . ."

Voice 2: Are you sure you wanted to use the word "ladies"?

Scene 2: A Presentation

Invited to read some of my poems, I accept. In the acceptance, fear begins. The pleasure of invitation meets the pressure of presentation.

Time passes; the event draws near. I face some simple decisions. I label the folder I plan to carry onstage: "Poems for Performance." My printed hand is too messy; the name is not quite right. "Start again," I say to myself, "using a different rubric, one where only I will know the code—what is concealed, what is assumed." I type, thinking of Yeats, "The Dancer" and stick it to the folder's tab. I want to believe that my labels can create reality. But, of course, we all have our fantasies.

I select certain poems, ones that I think I can present, ones that I think are presentable. But will these poems play well? Are they good poems? What or who are you featuring? What would be worse: "He's an adequate poet but not much of a performer," or "he's an adequate performer but not much of a poet"? My poet takes some comfort in my performer; my performer takes some comfort in my poet. Yet, no one is at ease.

I write transitional material. The goal is to sound clever, bright. Engage, entertain, and enlighten is the evaluative base. I try again. This time a new goal: Avoid embarrassment. Just say it so you aren't ashamed. Some lines get written—they will have to do for now. I must begin to rehearse.

I reserve a room for rehearsals. It is filled with equipment, overhead projectors, slide carousels, video cameras, tape recorders, music stands, and one enormous lectern. I approach it, place my notes, and look around. Empty chairs confront me. The room is silent as swallowed speech. I begin trying not to be heard beyond the walls. The silence between each phrase summons.

I try all the tricks I know—go over the poems again and again; I ask a friend for feedback; I rehearse in the clothes I plan to wear; I picture the audience members in their underwear; I tell the butterflies to fly in formation. As the presentation date draws near, rehearsals turn to chants for control—I think I can, I think I can, I think I can—my little red engine trying to believe it could.

The time arrives. I sit in front of the audience waiting for my turn. I don't hear what the speaker before me says. I look out. I see friendly faces, people I've known for years, friends who I know wish me well.

"I think I can," I say to myself. I'm introduced. I go to the lectern and open my folder.

My god! The words on the page blur. I can hardly see what I plan to read. I begin to speak, but my mind races down another track. What if I can't read the next word? Why did I use that phrasing? Why are those people whispering in the back? Am I speaking loudly enough? Why did I say I would do this? I hear myself stumble; I'm making a fool of myself. We are all embarrassed. My friends look down; the rest look away. I can't get back on track. The passengers are getting off this train. My god! Another mistake. What should I do now? Can I just stop here? Roll on. Soon you can unload this freight. Why is she smiling? What is he writing? A note for a friend? How long have I been up here? I am in a daze. Don't think. Just go on. In pain and exasperation, I reach the final stop and sit down.

Scene 3: Looking

Look at him. His hands are shaking. His voice is breaking. I hope he'll settle down. It isn't getting any better. If anything, worse. Oh, this is painful. Please get control of yourself. What will I be able to say to him when it's over? Put your notes down so they won't shake in your hands. There is no escape. I'll try to look supportive. Nod. Smile. I can't take much more of this. Oh, this will never end. Please just sit down. I can't look.

Scene 4: Looking Back

Look at them. When it works, it works. They are listening, being taken in, moved. They sit in my sweating palm.

Scene 5: High School Memories

One: I played the undertaker in *Our Town*. You may not remember the part; it's a small role in the final act. What I remember is being mistakenly made up in ghostly white as one of the dead and, then, since it was time for my entrance, having to go onstage. Whatever lines I had shared little resemblance to what I said. My grandmother's only remark was "He was out there for such a short amount of time, I almost missed him."

Two: I gave an oral report making fun of a children's book. I had them laughing, hooting, falling out their chairs. The teacher failed my effort arguing that I had not selected a text suitable for a high school reader. I was outraged, but I've never forgotten the sound of that audience.

Three: The upper grades were invited to watch the lower grades present their Christmas play. One little boy, dressed as a shepherd, had the task of providing a narrative transition between scenes. Once onstage, he became frightened. He gave all his lines, but as he did so, he twisted and twisted his robe until he created, unaware, the largest cloth penis I and the other howling audience members have ever seen. Remembering his confused face, I am ashamed I laughed. I ask for his forgiveness.

Four: I prepared a speech for the annual sports banquet. My charge was to thank the people who had worked with us. In my draft, I wrote: "I want to thank those wonderful people who have been so detrimental to our program." After rehearsing the speech in front of my best friend's mother, she asked if I really wanted to say "detrimental." She even, bless her, went to the trouble of looking up "detrimental" in the dictionary as if she wasn't sure what the word meant. No one could have handled the matter more delicately. Yet, in my mind I still see myself standing in front of an audience and telling them how detrimental our good coaches had been.

Scene 6: The Cures

Here are the cures: progressive relaxation, systematic desensitization, cognitive restructuring, therapy.

Tense, then relax those muscles, one group at a time. Again. Modify your behavior. Visualize evocative stimuli that may trouble. You can control the situation. Visualize yourself successfully completing the performative task. Substitute the positive for the negative. Replace irrational beliefs with rational ones.

Perhaps we need another session.

Scene 7: The Rewards

—vita line

—a nod in your direction

—a warm smile

—a few select words

—a hug

—power

Scene 8: Another Presentation

Approaching the lectern to give a paper on communication apprehension, a friend, reaching for a comic moment, asks if I'm nervous. I wasn't until then. I never know when it might come, when it might slip inside me. I stand outside myself watching. The choice is not mine. I may be invaded at any time. It may, like in *Alien*, push itself against my insides before it busts through. It may feed on me until I am a dried carcass. I long for a

Sigourney Weaver, bullet belts strapped across her chest and a gun in each hand, to blow it away. And let there be no sequels.

Scene 9: Dialogues

Person 1: Why do you do it if you don't want to?

Person 2: I don't have a choice. It's part of the job. Besides, sometimes it works.

Speaker 1: I get so angry when I get nervous. It just drives me crazy. I don't know why I get so nervous.

Speaker 2: Well, why don't you rehearse?

Speaker 1: I do.

Interactant 1: Did you see him?

Interactant 2: Yes, it was pathetic. I don't know why he gets so nervous.

He: It's a natural response.

She: It is?

Scene 10: The Research

Watson, Monroe, and Atterstrom:

> "Communication apprehension (CA), the fear of oral communication with another person or persons, is found to affect many individuals negatively by inhibiting amounts of communication and interfering with effectiveness in life experiences." (*Communication Quarterly* 37, 1989, 67)

No shit.

Aaron:

> "Stage fright intervenes in that gap between the actor as person and the actor as performer." (*Stage Fright: Its Role in Acting*, 130)

There is no gap.

McCroskey:

> "Extremely low CA can be just as abnormal as extremely high CA." (In Daly and McCroskey, eds., *Avoiding Communication*, 21)

But I bet it doesn't feel that way.

Jackson and Latane:

> "Stage fright or performance apprehension presumably reflects a fear of embarrassment. . . . the emotional distress of embarrassment is brought about by the fear that others are evaluating you negatively." (*Journal of Personality and Social Psychology* 40, 1981, 73)

And the fear that others are evaluating you positively.

McCroskey:

> "Communication apprehension (CA) has been the subject of over 200 reported studies during the decade of 1970–1980." (In *Communication Yearbook* 6, 1982)

Yea, and you wrote them all.

Ayres:

> "To minimize the development of CA students should be rewarded by teachers and others for engaging in communicative behavior. This is especially true in public speaking situations." (*Communication Research Reports* 5, 1988, 82)

That a boy, Ron, you just gave another line.

Pelias and Pelias:

> "In some cases, CA may be so acute that a student may be unable to complete the performance task." (*Communication Education* 37, 1988, 118)

What I'm trying to say is . . .

Beatty:

> "The long term effect of experiencing anxiety in public speaking situations is the development of predisposition to avoid communication." (*Communication Education* 37, 1988, 28)

"   "

84

Scene 11: The Body

Before	After
a dreading body, filled with promise	a pleased body, having gotten it done or gotten it done well
a taut body, ready and alert, watchful	a drained body, a calm and worthless carcass
an eliminating body, flushing the fluids of fear	a consuming body, hungry for the breaking of bread
a removed body, distanced, avoiding contact	an open vulnerable body, ready to take in what's given
a careful body, cautious and calculating	a free body, going with the flow
a planning body, rehearsing its final gesture	an improvisational body, greeting and seeking

Scene 12: The Dream

You are onstage and can't remember a single line. You try to ad-lib, but everyone gives you a puzzled look. You push on, but everything seems to be getting worse. You realize that you forgot to get dressed. The other actors try to cover for you, but you know that they are angry. The set begins to collapse around you. First, the door where you entered falls, framing you. Then, a wall comes down and then another one. You are standing in rubble. An actor approaches the audience and apologies for your actions, saying that you haven't been yourself lately, that they will clean up your mess and try to go on. You remain onstage, staring at your own nakedness.

Scene 13: Confessing to Friends

Buck up! Stop your whining. You know what to do. Just do it! Rehearse. Get yourself together. But please, stop your whining!

I don't mean to whine.

Maybe you're in the wrong field.

Scene 14: First Experiences

In kindergarten, our class would have a morning snack. We ate sitting on the floor, using our chairs as tables. I've lost the reason why we couldn't use our desks. Each child was directed to spread a white napkin, opened to a perfect square, on his/her chair, before two saltines would appear. Day in and day out, I was sure I wouldn't get it right.

I once gave a speech entitled "How to Swing a Golf Club." The embarrassment of that speech is not only its subject but a particular moment in the middle of the presentation. At the top of my swing, my knees began to shake so violently that I had to start walking to keep from falling down. It is difficult to teach the down swing in golf *while walking*.

Once, it went as planned: Hold steady. You're going to make it. This isn't too bad. Nobody knows. Just keep it up. You can get through it. A little bit at a time. You even got a laugh. Keep going. It's almost over. Just one more line to go. Smile. Give thanks. Amen. They were mine.

Scene 15: The Applause

There are two kinds: One acknowledges the effort, recognizes that the event took place. It may be polite, knowing the conventions of closure. It may be supportive, seeing the contract completed. It may be tired, thankful for the end. There is no shame in the polite, no embarrassment in the supportive. Their sound is safe, steady, sincere. But there is pain all around in the tired. It carries the sound of promises broken, of the soon forgotten, of an old man falling.

Two also acknowledges the effort, recognizes that the event took place, but it is ecstatic, celebratory, certain. It knows what it likes; it can stand on its own two feet. Its sound is full, as a single and sustained heartbeat, crowding out the air. Its sound is the tenor's song of spring. Its sound is the flugelhorn's orchestration.

That is the apprehensive's addiction. One could refuse the chance if one could.

Scene 16: Watching Others

They say everyone has it. With some, you can tell. With others, you can't. Sometimes, public confessions are made. Sometimes, you just wonder. Sometimes, you are amazed at the ease.

Scene 17: Another Presentation

They were all there—everyone I ever wanted to impress. It was a real opportunity just waiting for me. I took stage as if it were mine, as if fate were on my side. I knew what I had to do, and I knew I could do it. I had done it a thousand times in rehearsal:

I could do it in my sleep
I could do it while I sweep
I could do it standing up
I could do it on a cup
I could do it like a clown
I could do it upside down
I could do it eating green eggs and ham
I could do it playing Sam I am

I could do it until I saw them.

Scene 18: My Body

So far, there has been no sweating, no dry mouth, and no queasiness. First, it had the shakes—the hands fluttering, the knees knocking, the voice quivering. How can my body act without my intent? How can it refuse to go where it is told, to look where it is ordered? Then, it was the pounding—the heart racing in rhythm to the rapid speech and the breath disappearing in mid-phrase. Now, it goes deaf; it goes blind. It cannot hear what it says; it cannot see what it wrote.

Scene 19: The Aftermath

Some approach you and say it went well. You listen with hunger. You listen for the words you need to hear. You listen for the words that speak the truth, the words you can trust. Some simply leave. You believe them.

Epilogue

To end. To stop the eyes. The chance was taken. Let them judge if they must. Escape now to the comfort of silence. Regain your sight, your hearing. You have paid the price. Sit down. Listen to the sound of the applause.

8

The Audition

(The scene is the stage of a small theatre, bare except for a small wooden table and two chairs. The director [male or female] is a well-seasoned theatre practitioner, and the actor [male] is a young [20 to 30] aspiring performer.)

Director: Next. *(The actor enters and sits. The director examines the actor but says nothing.)*

Actor: Well, would you like me to do something?

Director: Do something?

Actor: Yes, you know. Read some part. I've brought some material. I can sing. I can dance, not great, mind you, but well enough to fit in any line.

Director: Sing and dance?

Actor: Yes. *(singing)* "Well, hello, Dolly. Well, hello, Dolly. It's so great to have you back where you belong. You're looking . . ."

Director: *(holds up hand to stop the actor from going on)*

Actor: Well, perhaps you could tell me what you're looking for. Do you have a particular type in mind? I do most accents: "Monsieur, may I be of service" or "We have our vays of making you talk." I'm very flexible. *(twisting his arm behind his head)* You'd be amazed. I can take on almost any shape. Perhaps I could read something from the script?

Director: It isn't set.

Actor: Oh, it's still being written. That's exciting. I love working with new material. With new stuff, you don't have to worry about other interpretations. That's why I hate performing Shakespeare. Everyone compares you to so-and-so's Hamlet or so-and-so's Othello. It's like you can't breathe. You're not doing Shakespeare, are you?

Director: No.

Actor: I was worried there for a minute. I mean I could do Shakespeare if you were doing Shakespeare. But I like new works the best. You are doing new material, right?

Director: It is always new.

Actor: Of course. I didn't mean to suggest that you would do something that wasn't original. After all, you are an artist. I mean that's why I want to work with you. I've heard what a wonderful director you are. It would be just a privilege to . . .

Director: *(holds up hand to stop the actor from going on)*

Actor: I'm not just saying that. I really mean it. I think it would be a privilege.

Director: What is a privilege?

Actor: Working with you.

Director: No. What is a privilege?

Actor: You want me to define the word "privilege"?

Director: Yes. Is that a problem for you?

Actor: No. I can define it. In this context, it's an opportunity, a chance given to just a few.

Director: An opportunity or chance for what?

Actor: To work with you.

Director: Sorry, I'm afraid you've got it wrong.

Actor: Wrong?

Director: Yes. *(silence for a considerable time, the director focusing on the actor)*

Actor: Perhaps I should just go. I'll just get my things and be out of your hair. *(starts to leave)*

Director: Don't you want a part?

Actor: Of course I do.

Director: Then let's start again. What is a privilege?

Actor: Acting?

Director: Acting?

Actor: Yes, acting. To take stage when the lights come up, to hear the applause. That's when I'm really alive.

Director: Are you dead on all other occasions?

Actor: No, not dead. I'm just not as . . . *(searching for a word)*

Director: Fulfilled?

Actor: Yes.

Director: Who does the filling?

Actor: The audience, I guess.

Director: Not you?

Actor: Well, I don't think I'm filling myself, if that's what you mean. But what I do is satisfying.

Director: Satisfying?

Actor: Yes, it's fulfilling.

Director: It fills you with what?

Actor: The joys of theatre.

Director: Oh, you can do better than that. You don't want that to be your answer, do you? You don't want me write that down on your audition sheet?

Actor: *(confused and exasperated)* What do you want?

Director: *(calm)* What do you want?

Actor: I want a part.

Director: Parts are for the taking.

Actor: I'll take one please.

Director: Which one?

Actor: How should I know? You haven't even said what the play is about?

Director: What would you like it to be about?

Actor: Christ! This is crazy.

Director: Would you like it to be about your life?

Actor: My life?

Director: Yes.

Actor: Not much drama there. It's the same old story: Boy gets bit in the butt by the acting bug. Looks for roles. Finds some but can hardly make a living. He waits tables between parts.

Director: *(continuing the story)* His career is his top priority. He will do anything to be a star. He becomes self-absorbed. He forgets his friends, except those who might help him. He ruins all relationships by either avoiding intimacy or forcing his partner into the supportive mother role. He never gets offstage. All he wants is to make it big.

Actor: I know that script, but it's not mine.

Director: Really?

Actor: Really.

Director: I would be honored to know your script.

Actor: Privileged?

Director: Yes, privileged.

Actor: Wait, I get it. You're doing some psychodrama thing where all the actors pour out their guts, tell the horrors of their lives. Well, I don't have any horrors. I came from a family filled with love.

Director: Filled?

Actor: Yes, there is no question about it. We will always be there for each other.

Director: There?

Actor: Well, of course, not literally. I'm here, and they're in Missouri. But, you know, a presence in each other's lives.

Director: Yes.

Actor: Once I had this small role as a gay guy dying of AIDS, and my father and mother came to see the show. Now, they aren't theatre people. They're farmers. Twenty minutes after the show, I found my father still sitting with my mother in the theatre, crying. At first I thought he was crying about the show. But the show wasn't much of a tear jerker. Then I was worried that something else was wrong. When he saw me, he started crying louder and took me in his arms. "Don't die. Don't die," he kept saying, over and over. "I'm not, Papa," I said, "I was only playing a part." Then, he pulled back to look me in the eyes and spoke: "If you're gay, that's alright. We can accept that."

Director: Are you gay?

Actor: No. I tried it, but it's not my thing.

Director: Do your parents know you're straight?

Actor: They won't believe me. They keep telling me that it's fine with them if I'm gay, that I ought to bring some of my friends home for them to meet. Mom says she could use someone with a good decorating eye.

Director: I see. Your parents deeply love a character you once played. That's what fulfills them.

Actor: No, they love me.

Director: Have they seen you in any other show?

Actor: No.

Director: Then they have found who they want to love.

Actor: Must we continue this?

Director: No. You brought them up.

Actor: I did?

Director: Yes.

Actor: Why do you suppose?

Director: Need.

Actor: Need?

Director: And privilege.

Actor: Is that what the show is about?

Director: Do you think so?

Actor: Yes.

Director: Whose need and privilege?

Actor: Mine.

Director: Only in part.

Actor: What are the other parts?

Director: Who else needs a part?

Actor: Must we continue in riddles? Can't you just say what you want?

Director: Can you?

Actor: I said I wanted a part. Actually, I need a part. It's been a while since I've worked. If you look at my audition sheet, you'll see that I have lots of experience. I know I could do what you want, whatever that is. I need a part.

Director: You already have one.

Actor: You mean I've been cast.

Director: No.

Actor: My god! I guess you want me to grovel.

Director: Do you want the part of the groveler?

Actor: Is that one of the roles?

Director: It isn't set. But sometimes, that is what is needed.

Actor: Well, I can grovel, but I don't find it very becoming. It seems to alter my best side.

Director: What is your best side?

Actor: *(posing)* Can't you tell?

Director: We seem to have taken a step back.

Actor: We have?

Director: Yes. What is your best side away from the mirror?

Actor: Well, I'm kind to our furry friends, and I've never murdered anyone, and I'm . . .

Director: *(holds up hand to stop the actor from going on)* You have never murdered anyone?

Actor: Of course not! What a question!

Director: You brought it up. I think we should pursue it.

Actor: Pursue what?

Director: Who you have murdered.

Actor: I've never murdered anyone!

Director: Are you sure?

Actor: I think that is something I'd remember.

Director: Perhaps, but I think we need details.

Actor: Details about what?

Director: Your murders.

Actor: This is ridiculous. I came in here to audition, not to play these games. Now what exactly would you like me to do?

Director: Tell me about your murders. Have you ever killed a scene?

Actor: Well, if that's what you mean, sure. Hasn't everybody?

Director: Tell me about it.

Actor: Let me think. There was this play I did in college. I can't even remember the name of it, but it was awful. I was playing this character who sells his soul for the ability to see into the future. He learns about the future by reading newspapers that have not yet been published. He makes a fortune, gets everything he wants. Then, one day reading the paper, he sees his obituary. I had the line "Shocking to read such a thing," and then I had to die immediately thereafter. No matter how I did it, the audience would always laugh.

Director: What other characters have you killed?

Actor: I can't think of any others.

Director: Characters who have been smothered in your bag of tricks, characters who you performed without a second thought, characters who you never bothered to meet?

Actor: There are times, perhaps, that I relied upon my craft to carry me through. But if you gave me a part, I would give it my best.

Director: Your best side?

Actor: No, I mean my best effort.

Director: Then, there were times when you didn't give your best effort?

Actor: I guess.

Director: Times when you didn't think there was a need?

Actor: Yes, I suppose.

Director: Times when you forgot the privilege?

Actor: Yes.

Director: I see. *(The director writes on the actor's audition sheet.)*

Actor: What are you writing? You can't keep me from having a part because of what I just said.

Director: I can't?

Actor: It wouldn't be fair.

Director: Were you fair?

Actor: Okay, okay, I'm out of here. I'm through with all this. You can do your thing with someone else. I'm history. *(starts to leave)*

Director: Would you silence yourself?

Actor: Silence myself?

Director: Yes. Do you want the part where you are not heard?

Actor: Is it a good part?

Director: Not very.

Actor: Then I don't want it.

Director: Then you should stay.

Actor: And do what?

Director: Tell me who you would silence.

Actor: No one.

Director: Be careful how you answer. You were just about to silence yourself. If you would silence yourself, wouldn't you silence others?

Actor: Not intentionally.

Director: Unintentionally?

Actor: Who knows?

Director: Don't you?

Actor: I don't know.

Director: Why not?

Actor: Because I've never had to know.

Director: Good! *(writes on actor's audition sheet)*

Actor: Good?

Director: Yes. That was an excellent answer.

Actor: It was?

The Audition

Director: Yes. Let's begin again. Tell me about acting.

Actor: *(tentative)* It's a privilege.

Director: Yes.

Actor: *(still tentative)* It's a necessity.

Director: Yes, and?

Actor: And I really need this part.

Director: *(writing on audition form)* For a moment I thought we were getting somewhere.

Actor: Are you disappointed in my answer? I was just being truthful.

Director: Truthful?

Actor: Yes. I do need this part.

Director: Why?

Actor: To eat.

Director: Sorry, there are no parts for cannibals.

Actor: How do you know if it isn't set?

Director: My job is to keep cannibals from the stage.

Actor: And you think I'm a cannibal?

Director: To be blunt, yes. But you may take this opportunity to answer the charge.

Actor: You want me to defend myself?

Director: If you wish.

Actor: I'm not sure I do. You'll just turn what I say into another of your questions. You'll twist whatever I say against me. And I've done nothing wrong. I just want to act. I've always wanted to act. To be onstage, that's what matters. To have the lights come up and there you are. Everyone looking, waiting for you to speak. And when you're on, they're like children eating from your hands. Perhaps I haven't made the most out of every opportunity, but who has? Who can honestly say "I did my best every time"?

Director: What is your best?

Actor: *(posing)* My left.

Director: I believe we're through.

Actor: *(frustrated)* What would you like me to say? I can sing and dance. What would you like me to do?

Director: Nothing. We're finished. Thank you for auditioning.

Actor: Wait. It can't end like this. I think I'm getting it. I think I know what you want. Just give me a few more minutes.

Director: What else would you like to say?

Actor: You said I could have the part of the unheard.

Director: Yes. That is how I've cast you.

Actor: I think I've played that role before.

Director: Yes. But you failed to bring any sense of responsibility to the part.

Actor: Oh, if you give me a different part, I'll be responsible.

Director: You are not ready. You do not understand. Next.

9

Becoming Another: A Love Song for J. Alfred Prufrock

I select a poem I have long known and long loved: T. S. Eliot's "The Love Song of J. Alfred Prufrock." I remember certain lines, images, and J. Alfred Prufrock, the speaker of the poem. I do not, however, have much sense of the poem's movement, its structure, its logic. I do not know how the lines connect, how the attitudes shift, how the character unfolds. I do not have the poem committed to memory. Most of all, I do not have a sense of the other living within my body. I want to use the five steps of playing, testing, choosing, repeating, and presenting as a rehearsal procedure for becoming another. I have been exploring these steps for some time now. I know they overlap, circle around and cut through each other, confuse any simple linear scheme, but they offer me some guiding landmarks, places where I want to stop, places I need to visit. I begin by getting up and reading aloud.

Playing

Too much rushes in on first reading. I feel open, receptive, ready to discover what the poem gives. But so many possibilities suggest themselves: I hear possible line readings; I note details of Prufrock's character; I see potential scenes; I speculate about whether the "you" is an onstage or offstage or imaginary audience; I recognize certain sounds and rhythms; I even try some physical actions, some blocking.

I decide to pursue character first. If I can find Prufrock, I will have moved into the heart of the poem. I restrict myself on the next reading to finding all the ways Prufrock describes himself. I skim, noting Prufrock's physical traits: "balding," wearing a "morning coat" (collar to chin) and "necktie" ("rich," "modest," "asserted by simple pin"), thin. "Balding," no problem; "thin," a problem if I want a physical match. I'll consider wearing a coat and tie as possible costume pieces, perhaps, creating the turn of the century, the probable historical period of the poem. I make a note to check with the costumer.

I know that physical traits are only a small part of the equation, so I turn to questions of attitude, personality, feelings. I am drawn to some of my favorite lines. I read, "And time yet for a hundred indecisions, / And time for a hundred visions and revisions." Prufrock is someone who would not "dare to eat a peach." I recognize the irony that this indecisive, frightened, cautious person says he is "no Prince Hamlet," "no prophet," as if one might assume he was. Instead, I trust Prufrock when he says of himself: "I have measured out my life with coffee spoons." He is a man who questions whether he should "roll his trousers" or "part his hair behind," who feels as if he "should have been a pair of ragged claws / Scuttling across the floors of silent seas." He is a man who sees himself "formulated, sprawling on a pin" under the scrutinizing eyes of the women who "come and go / Talking of Michelangelo."

With this as a starting point, I am back on my feet. I try saying the poem as Prufrock, as an insecure, nervous person, fearful of human contact. I learn much. One, I cannot sustain that persona for the length of the poem without boring the audience and myself and, more importantly, without making the audience dislike Prufrock. Played throughout as insecure and fearful, Prufrock seems as if he is just whining about his plight. He must do more than snivel; he must be someone with whom the audience can identify. Two, many of the lines point to other aspects of Prufrock—his ability to command language, creating such vivid images in, for instance, the fog stanza; his fantasies, such as when he hears the mermaids singing or imagines what others might say; his critique of prevailing social affairs, trivial, vacuous, and cruel events where people "come and go / Talking of Michelangelo" while sizing up others. Three, the rhythm of many lines resists a halting and hesitant voice. The quick internal and end rhymes, the flowing iambic lines, the smooth assonance and alliteration, and the repetition of words and phrases encourage a quicker pace than one associates with cautious and nervous speech.

I decide to try again, this time assuming that Prufrock is a humble, disillusioned dreamer. My attempt seems inadequate. The "humble, disillusioned dreamer" character does not hold steady. The disillusioned dreamer seems too bitter, too cynical in my rendering. Again, I have created a speaker no one could like. I lost much of the humble dreamer I wanted in the articulation, but I sense that with rehearsal I can create such a character. I do that character well enough, however, to know that I have not captured all of Prufrock. That character misses his ineptness, misses his desire for human contact. After all, this is Prufrock's "love song." He is motivated by his need for love. He is driven to find his mermaid.

Or is it his lament, his ode for our symbolic drowning? We travel with Prufrock, told from the first line to come along, placed in the social scene (e.g., "Time for you and time for me" and "Stretched on the floor, here beside you and me"), and linger with him in the final stanza "in the chambers of the sea / . . . Till human voices wake us, and we drown." Like Prufrock, we are, as the epigraph from Dante's *Inferno* suggests, caught in the underworld, never to be alive to this world again. Like Prufrock, we are unable to connect with one another in any meaningful way. Thus, Prufrock is, as Eliot would explain, an objective correlative, a stand-in for emotions we have all known.

I feel ready to test the proposition that Prufrock is a humble, inept, disillusioned dreamer who seeks genuine human contact and wants to teach us about the difficulties of establishing such relationships. Other matters, however, insist on attention first. In particular, it seems essential to play with some options that (1) would define the audience by specifying the "you" in the poem and (2) would establish questions of scene.

I try suggesting that I am speaking to someone onstage, an imaginary person who is following me along as I travel through the scenes. I reject the idea quickly—it looks silly and confusing. I consider casting another person in the role of "you." I reject this idea just as quickly—it would pull too much attention from Prufrock. I do not want to feature the relationship between Prufrock and some anonymous other. I know I must speak directly to the attending audience, must make them into the "you." I can see myself moving toward them, moving away. They will serve as useful anchor points, points of departure and return.

But from where am I departing, where am I going, where do I return? The questions, I realize, depend upon the degree to which I want to literalize the social scene, to suggest that Prufrock is literally taking part in the social event. On one end of the continuum, I consider a complete set, finely appointed and filled with detail. This scene, as I envision it, would necessitate having a number of people milling about, costumed, engaged in social chatter. The impracticality of this option is sufficient reason for its rejection. On the other end of the continuum, I can see Prufrock simply sitting, talking directly to the audience, psychologically attuned to their reactions to what he is saying. I decide that this option is worth a try. I learn two important things: (1) I do not trust my vocal abilities as a performer to sustain interest in a poem of that length without movement; and (2) saying certain lines with the assumption that Prufrock is highly conscious of his audience seems to work particularly well. I tentatively settle upon using the stage space to suggest shifts in scene and changes in Prufrock's relationship to his audience. Blocking will emerge from these premises.

Through playing, then, I gained some broad ideas about the character, audience, and scene I want to pursue. I am beginning to get a feel for the poem, beginning to know Prufrock, but he still seems far removed, a mere acquaintance. He stands at a distance as I look on. I want to move closer. I want his language to be mine. I want to test my hunches.

Testing

I need to place my playful speculations against the poem and against my abilities. I need to discover if what I believe about Prufrock will hold still so that it might grow in complexity and depth. I need to find what I can do, what skills I must call upon or develop in order to enact my vision. In short, I need to build a case that I can present. I am back on my feet.

The first time through Prufrock comes off much too strong, forceful, too much in control. The next time he appears too weak, incapable, too much of a pathetic figure. I remain convinced, however, that he has moments of strength and weakness. I need to make some decisions about each stanza, each line. I go over the first stanza. I struggle first to find a wording that makes sense, that clarifies some tricky lines. Once settled, I pursue the stanza, giving Prufrock strength. I am even able to put off any question the audience might have: "Oh, do not ask, 'What is it?' / Let us go and make our visit." His language, though, is also filled with negative images—"half-deserted streets," "restless nights," "one-night cheap hotel," "tedious argument / Of insidious intent"—setting the tone for the poem and providing the initial glimpse into his disillusionment. I discover that I can capture Prufrock's strength and disillusionment with blocking. By focusing upon and moving toward the audience on the lines that directly reference them, I give Prufrock some command of the situation. By turning away from the audience and seeing the scene onstage, the images of darkness, of shadows and silhouettes, of forbidding streets, seem to take shape.

I perform the opening stanza several times, each time feeling more confident in my choices, each time more secure that the choices are workable. That is, I trust that my interpretation is a valid one and that, with rehearsal, I can do in performance what I need to do. As I move on, I face a seemingly radical shift in attitude from stanza one, to two, to three. How does Prufrock move from telling the audience "let us go and make out visit" (stanza one) to immediately seeing "the women come and go / Talking of Michelangelo" (stanza two) to the description of "the yellow fog that rubs its back upon the window-panes" (stanza three)?

I discover my answer in the performance paradigm of psychological realism, a paradigm I have been evoking without reflection until this moment. I pause to consider if an alternative performance style might work, something highly stylized that breaks from a realistic rendering of character. I allow myself to play along these lines for a short period but determine that I have invested too much already to start down an alternative path. I return to thinking how Prufrock, after telling the audience to come visit, is struck with an image of the women coming and going at the social event, an event that frightens him and makes him hesitant to proceed. He delays the journey with his description of the "soft October night."

I am convinced of the potential of this logic when I perform the second stanza with my eyes closed. The image of women become Prufrock's private terror, etched in his mind as a memory of his failure. When I close my eyes in performance on those lines, I see the women vividly. I feel the desire to shut them out. I feel as if I want to turn away. My face grimaces and my body tightens before I remember that I must return to my audience, that I must not forget their presence. Prufrock's private fear slips into the conversation like a slap. I recover by speaking of fog. Perhaps, though, I could read the second stanza to suggest that Prufrock has arrived with his listeners at the scene. The fog surrounds the social gathering, holding everyone together in empty rituals. When I try this possibility in performance, it seems to work against the future tense of the poem, a detail I had overlooked until now. Perhaps Prufrock never arrives, is never literally in the scene. I try performing as if the entire piece takes place in Prufrock's imagination. That seems to be a workable option. I'll have to make a decision about how I want to play this.

I proceed throughout the entire poem in a similar manner, testing, probing my hunches, discovering new ideas, using blocking to clarify and to uncover certain insights, exploring my performance potential, playing again, experimenting. I mark the script, indicating attitude shifts, specifying blocking options, and noting difficulties in performance execution. I have taken a step closer to Prufrock. I've come to understand his logic, his motivation as he moves from one point to another, his through line. I have also begun to experience his voice and body as different from my own but residing within me. I begin to speak of myself as Prufrock, making his pronouns my own.

I, as Prufrock, begin to speak in the first person singular.

Choosing

Confident I am generally on the right tract, I know I must begin to select the options I want to keep. I need to start making some definite decisions. From the many legitimate possibilities before me, I need to commit to certain choices. Some decisions, by working within certain parameters, just happen—the phrasing of a line, the gesture to hide Prufrock's bald spot, the slight mimicking of the quoted voices, and so on. Subconsciously tested by the body, these decisions just fall in place. They are choices, never articulated, that just feel right. They come, perhaps, from inviting a character to live within you. They come, perhaps, from doing performances, over and over, through the years, until you begin to trust your body.

Other decisions are highly conscious. They are carefully considered based upon aesthetic judgments. I alter an earlier decision when I come to recognize, for example, that closing my eyes during stanza two is not a happy aesthetic choice—it feels too big, too melodramatic. I select instead a smaller action, a slight glance away, to achieve the effect I want. In part guided by the performance principle of "less is more," I opt for the minimal gesture and sense the stillness pulling the audience in. Feeling the seductive power of stillness, I decide to play most of the first three stanzas stationary, quite erect, arms often locked behind, within a small pool of light. The reticent and disillusioned Prufrock, I believe, would fill very little space. I know, too, that after the three stanzas, I need to move. The power of that stillness is lost if I try to sustain it for too long a time.

Even though I have elected not to literalize the scene, because of the technical problems associate with getting props, costumes, and other actors, I decide to dress in a morning coat. I do not want my dress to locate the scene at a particular historical moment and perhaps undermine the currency of the poem for a contemporary audience. It is essential, I believe though, to establish some formality. Furthermore, I do not want to cut or to play against the specific reference to a morning coat in the poem. Complementing the morning coat, I decide to work with an elegant, slightly faded Victorian chair and a small pillow.

I first let my body enact the actions of the fog, rubbing, licking, slipping around the "soft October night." Then I try having my hands suggest the fog, moving them in keeping with the fog's actions. Neither choice works. They feel forced, staged. The actions do not feel right in my body. I simply do not trust that Prufrock would embody such behaviors. I do get from trying these choices, however, a greater sense of the sensuousness of the stanza. While I reject these actions as viable performance options, I learn from doing them the seductive and descriptive power of the stanza. I decide simply to see the fog in front of and around me and to cross my arms on the final line of the stanza, "Curled once about the house, and fell asleep." This performance choice seems to work and, as a consequence of trying the other options, seems quite alive bodily. It seems alive without being over-wrought.

I discover that I can push myself against the back of the chair, sitting erect and stretching my arms up around the sides, to give the impression that I "am pinned and wriggling on the wall." I find that sitting on the arm of the chair feels too casual, and I deny myself that option. I realize that coming completely out of the chair on "I am Lazarus, come from the dead" is less effective than simply moving to the edge of the seat before settling back on "'That is not what I meant at all. / That is not it, at all.'" I learn it feels right to suggest Prufrock's fear by moving into the chair on "And in short, I was afraid."

I decide that the final five stanzas need a considerable amount of performance time. They serve as closure to the poem, summarizing familiar themes and ending in despair. They are all short stanzas, progressing with a 2, 3, 1, 3, 3 line pattern, that take us to Prufrock's fantasy mermaid world. The single line stanza presents a Prufrock who cannot find happiness even in his own fantasies: "I do not think that they will sing to me." With us, he awaits "Till human voices wake us, and we drown." The short stanzas here suggest a disjointed, fragmented reality, one where we join an aging Prufrock, resigned to failure. To settle into such attitudes, I need time, time to move from one idea to another, time to suggest age, time to feel the emptiness, time to reach without being able to grasp, time to drown.

I decide to make the Prince Hamlet stanza the climactic point in the poem. Prufrock is at his most animated here, fully drawn as an "attendant lord," as "the Fool." The rhythm of the lines emerge quickly by paying attention to their endings and punctuation. I want the rhythm within the stanza to build until Prufrock describes himself as "the Fool." Within a few readings, my choices feel fixed. I kowtow on "Am an attendant lord," bending at the waist with a submissive nod. I swell, inhaling on "full of high sentence," and release, exhaling on "a bit obtuse." I color the adjectives to set up the final one, "almost ridiculous." It is a fun stanza to do: easy to remember, easy to enact, easy to make work. The stanza, ironically, is a climax where I can rest, trusting in my ability to pull if off, confident that I can become Prufrock at that moment. I wonder, however, if my choices are too easy, too predictable, too obvious, but I move on, remembering Prufrock's lines: "time yet for a hundred indecisions, / And for a hundred visions and revisions."

But with each decision, Prufrock is being built, made of my own construction. Some gestures that I discard I know are not his; some I sense he would not do just at that moment; some I simply forget. Some gestures that I keep just seem predictable, common to a given utterance. Others are more telling, unique to Prufrock, indicating his character. His body is becoming mine. I hear his voice speaking within me. But he slips away, forgets what he wants to say, breaks into old ways of being. Prufrock, stay with me.

Repeating

I must make his words mine. I must control them, own them, know that they will be there. The beginning and ending of the poem come quickly. The middle shifts about with its repetitions—e.g., "Do I dare?" "How should I presume?" "There will be time." It refuses to hold still. With some lines, I invert the sequence; with others, I drop words or phrases;

with still others, I forget them altogether. I even change the order of two stanzas, a switch that every time I do it leaves me lost, scrambling for the script. I set aside a day just to memorize, to ensure the language is mine.

This is both my least and most favorite time in rehearsal. I become angry when I forget. I feel frustrated. I say the lines, over and over, searching for mnemonic devices. At times, I am bored and have to force myself to concentrate. At times, I just don't want to go on. I think of reasons for not working. I try to convince myself that I know it when I don't. I daydream. I act silly, reciting lines in different accents, different pitches, different characters. I am removed from Prufrock. I am a mere technician putting in the right wiring.

But, at times, the wiring connects. I see things I never saw before. Without the script in hand, my body becomes free. It moves in ways it never has before. I find myself playing once again, testing possibilities, choosing among them. My body is speaking, guiding me to new discoveries. My body is becoming his. I am learning how it feels when it speaks, how it moves in space, how it looks at others. I move away as the "women come and go," feeling like a "Pair of ragged claws / Scuttling across the floors of silent seas," anxious not to intrude, not to get in the way. I stand outside the scene, commenting but never entering it, and become an "attendant lord," solicitous, nodding and bowing, never center stage. I struggle to find words and to make eye contact with the audience, sensing myself as a frustrated guide, "Lazarus, come from the dead, / Come back to tell you all," who feels "It is impossible to say just what I mean!"

I begin to hear what is being said by listening to my own utterances. I hear the harsh anger and disgust in my voice as I say, "spit out all the butt-ends of my days and ways." I feel the longing for contact by reciting, "Is it perfume from a dress / That makes me so digress?" I listen to the cold dismissal as I repeat the lines, "That is not it at all, / That is not what I meant, at all." I come to know in the saying. My voice is speaking to me, making me listen, pulling me closer to Prufrock. The bodily and vocal wires linking me to Prufrock become so intertwined that our separate identities blur. There are literally thousands of connecting points, points where voice and body transform into a common circuit. We become two generating sources, alternating currents, charged, creating voltage. Still, however, each time I pull the switch, the meter fluctuates.

I must become more consistent. Prufrock's possibilities, though, never stop unfolding. I want the piece set, but I still keep finding options I like, small, subtle things I want to incorporate. Many things are holding still. The blocking seems fixed, aiding me in memorization. The broad attitude shifts, and bodily behaviors appear firm. This keeps my through line in place and establishes the central aspects of Prufrock's character. What shifts are issues of pace, intensity, weight? Should I say this line quicker, throwing it away? Should I speak louder on this phrase, giving it more emphasis? Should I stress this word, investing it with more weight? Should I move more closely to the audience on the final stanza, allowing them to become more fully implicated? I answer such questions on feel. I trust myself to make the right choices without having to articulate why. My answers come from what has come before, in the flow of the moment, from my state of being. My answers come somatically, in my corporeal presence. My answers come as ineffable gifts.

Yet, I feel a need for some feedback. I need an outside eye. I ask a colleague to come to a rehearsal, and when she agrees, I sense a rush of adrenaline. Imagined audiences cannot compete with real ones. Another's presence raises the stakes. Moving from a private affair to a public one, I feel accountable, vulnerable, apologetic. What I have come to value may not measure up, may not be worthy of a witness. What I have worked on, trusted, and believed in will be scrutinized, pushed this way and that, reworked. My fragile love affair with Prufrock must come under the authoritative eye of a critic. Despite being impatient with my students when they engage in such behaviors, I offer disclaimers, words designed to lower expectations, in the hopes that my witness, not expecting much, will say: "That was wonderful! I don't know why you were apologizing." I know better than to think this will or should happen, but the desire remains. I feel anger at my own need for approval, particularly at this point in the rehearsal process. How immature! How unprofessional! I feel exposed.

We begin. She writes something on her white pad before I'm finished the first line. I'm distracted but regain concentration. Playing to this audience of one, I cannot stop watching her reactions, when she writes, when she smiles or frowns, when she seems to be taken in. I want her to see certain performance moments, moments I think work particularly well. I'm disappointed when, during those times, her pad commands her attention. I want to say, "I'll stop until you write what you need to so that you can see what I'm doing." But I push on. Prufrock unwinds on an automatic tape, made from days of rehearsal. I am too aware of myself as a performer, too aware of my witness, too aware of Prufrock simply going through the motions. When I finish, I resist apologizing yet again.

On the white pad before her are two pages of notes, written in small letters. Those pages, swirling with response, contain a verdict. They exist before me as a plate of food before a starving man. She and I both know that I must be fed with care. She says, "I'll be blunt," knowing that bluntness suggests both candor and a dulled edge. "Good," I respond, knowing that I have no choice but to accept what is given. I cannot be defensive. I cannot protect myself. I must, instead, welcome what may sicken, what may cure.

Some of her comments place a question mark between Prufrock and me. They linger inside, instilling doubt. They make me suspicious of what I once trusted. The seams that once connected are stretched, ready to rip apart. Having been questioned, my relationship to Prufrock changes. It is as if a friend hinted at some hidden secret, alluded to some buried skeleton I would have never discovered on my own. I will have to examine our relationship. I will have to work with Mr. Prufrock before we can be as we once were, comfortable, intimate, at peace.

Some of her comments burst out, exclaiming what works and what does not. They are moments I trust without question. They come without reasons, without thought, popping out like a knee coming out of joint. I remember them in the days that come. They are icons of assessment, emotions laid bare. They serve to solidify or eliminate choices, as one might when shopping for the perfect gift.

Some of her comments declare truths, obdurate facts that need attention. They are new markers for the road, charting the right path. These maps, indicating features that cannot be missed if I had only looked, name the geography. They identify twists and turns and note points of interest. They are moments of embarrassment, moments when the tourist tells the tour guide about the terrain.

Some of her comments become imperatives: "You must . . . , you should not . . . , you have to . . ." These are rules to follow if I am to get it right. These orders mandate action, prescribe behaviors. These commandments do not bend or give; they are set, secure as a scout's knot. They cannot be breached without breaching the contract that invited her responses. Once established, they become benchmarks, permanent reference points, etched on the body.

In the end, I see Prufrock differently. Not only, with the aid of an outside eye, do I discover or remember other aspects of Prufrock—his lament might be viewed as sniveling unbecoming a man, his insights emerge from a compelling wit and intelligence, and so on—but I also find my relationship to him changed. While not a stranger, he seems strange. It is as if he said something or disclosed some private matter that makes me want to rethink what I thought I knew, to reestablish contact, to reaffirm our intimacy. I want again a level of trust, a space where there are no secrets or surprises.

In the end, I alter performance choices. I take away a breathy quality I was unaware I was using on certain lines. I clarify the scenes to show in greater detail when Prufrock is living in actual or remembered space. I change focus, looking more often directly at the audience. I push Prufrock's competencies in front of his incompetencies. I allow him to surrender more fully to the sensuousness of the fog stanza. I slow down between most stanzas, allowing attitudinal shifts to read as more clearly motivated. I downplay the lyrical quality of the poem in order to keep Prufrock from appearing self-absorbed, to stop his whining. I take time, as Prufrock would say, "for a hundred indecisions, / And for a hundred visions and revisions, / before the taking of a toast and tea." In short, I am playing, testing and choosing once again. I do so, again and again, in large and subtle ways, until it is time to present. And again, as Prufrock would say, "I have seen the moment of my greatness flicker / . . . / And in short, I was afraid."

In the end, I am reminded of who I am, a middle-aged, mediocre performer "with a bald spot in the middle of my hair," "one that will do . . . [to] start a scene or two," perhaps, advise a player, "politic" "but a bit obtuse," "indeed, almost ridiculous," indeed, "at times, the Fool."

Presenting

I awake the morning of the performance agitated, my body tired from the tossing and turning of the night before. I do my morning routine, reciting, yet again, my lines. I am pleased—no dropped lines or forgotten phrases. I continue my day, filled with the ordinary business of teaching, appointments, and meetings, distracted. I never forget that I'm scheduled to perform that afternoon, and I find time for a late morning rehearsal. It goes well. I feel ready.

After a light lunch, I walk to the theatre earlier than necessary, check the stage to ensure everything is in order, and wait in silence, surprised that I am calm. The silence is broken when they enter, almost, it seems, all at once. Some nod greetings or exchange pleasantries with me. Of the four faculty members scheduled to perform for the faculty performance hour, I am slated to go on third. It begins, and I try to focus on the first two presentations with limited success. When I hear the applause following the second performer, I join in, but knowing I'm next, my body, flush with the moment, burns. I take a deep breath and go onstage.

I look out and see them looking. They are ready, perhaps even eager. I call for Prufrock. I ask him to come and we begin, mechanically at first, but soon we are moving as one, moving as if I'm a minute figure riding on Prufrock's shoulder, watching him, listening to him speak. Mostly, I ride in silence, but at times, I whisper to Prufrock—"You did that well. Good for you!" "Don't forget to cross here." "Look at the woman in the second row." Only once do my whisperings make Prufrock stumble.

Under the gaze, I proceed. Some eyes appear tender as tulips caught in a late spring snow. They are with Prufrock, soft as a trembling heart. Some encompass the moment, encircling another world. They are steady, focused, ubiquitous as Mona Lisa's. Some are shy, averting an encounter, glancing from the side. They refuse, despite their desire, to connect.

Some look bored and search here and there for anything of interest. Tired and tumid, they roam the theatre as if they are at the end of a twenty-one-day tour. A few seem hostile, enraged and reckless as a trapped animal desperate for escape. They see ripped flesh before them.

It ends and I hear applause—sincere, I believe. I return to my seat pleased it is over. I am relieved. I feel my body begin to loosen, muscles relax, and I gain weight, becoming heavy with the finality of it all. I replay in my mind certain moments of my performance and make assessments. I believe I performed as well as I am able, which is to say, the performance was adequate, even, I allow myself to think, without embarrassment. Prufrock has dropped out of my reflections—my thoughts are about me, about me as a public performer offering up what I am able. I cannot focus on the last performer.

I empower those who listened as I wait hungrily for their response, their verdict. I feel ashamed that I crave their approval. I have been around theatre long enough to know how people speak following a performance and long enough not to trust such talk. I adopt a strategy to appear gracious: "Oh, you were wonderful!" "Thanks," I say in reply, "It's a wonderful poem. I just loved working on it." Against my genuine desire, I move the talk away from me and onto the poem. But, despite knowing better, I hang on their words and watch their expressions. I gather everything in as if I were trying to sweep all the talk into neat little piles, piles I can manage. I am a child. I want to go home and hide under my bed.

In the days and months that follow, I crawl out and Prufrock comes with me. He is always within call, always present when needed. He gives me words to think, words to say, words to script my life. He says to me when I make my morning coffee, "I have measured out my life with coffee spoons." He whispers when I am indecisive, "There will be time, there will be time." He nudges me at certain pressing moments, "And would it have been worth it, after all"? He reminds me, "It is impossible to say just what I mean."

10

Performance Is . . .

Performance is
> a way of giving shape to haunting spirits, putting into form what disturbs, what fascinates, what demands attention; that is, performance is a way of formulating the unforgettable so that it might be forgotten.

Performance is
> an act of becoming, a strategy for discovering oneself by trying on scripts to test their fit, a means of clothing oneself in various languages until one believes what one says.

Performance is
> a choice, a swirling possibility among many that refuses to hold still, a momentary investment, suddenly appearing and spinning away like spring.

Performance is
> a desire for the ineffable, to say what cannot be said by placing one's soul on the tongue, by sacrificing through discipline and prayer, by trusting the sheer luck or magic that beckons one to dance in the playground of angels.

Performance is
> the mundane activity of being, actions, familiar as peas, that take us through the day, always filled with personal significance, always insignificant, always a step closer to our final soliloquy.

Performance is
> an option, free from biological and cultural constraints, that transcends race, class, and gender because belief can make it so, because belief can reach beyond itself, because belief can set its anchor anywhere.

Performance is
> communication, a negotiated encounter elbowing its way into meaning, a place where words want to be heard, a place where speech struggles out and censors listen.

Performance is
> an invitation with embossed print, placed in the theatrical envelope, sealed by one's presence and designed to sanctify the ceremony of giving.

Performance is

therapy that traces years in carbon, duplicating the pleasures and pains of life as if to live again will allow all to settle like seagulls landing; therapy that announces one's illness: a patient prostrate on the stage floor, humble and hurried, scrutinized like a disease; therapy that cures the sick and the curious.

Performance is

a method of understanding, bodily, located in the experience of doing— as the carpenter knows the weight of the hammer, as the sculptor feels the smoothness of the stone, as the child learns the tricks of the tree.

Performance is

a commodity, brought and sold, a business of flesh, displayed for the passing pleasure of the consumer, displayed for the masters of the gaze, displayed like breasts.

Performance is

a vacant space, filled with possibilities, where the lion waits and the vulture sits still in anticipation, ready for their day's fare, ready for their ration, ready for sustenance.

Performance is

a personal expression, a pressing for voice, a pressing against silence until one pushes onstage to assert "I am, I am" as the lights fade: Expression leads to oppression, oppression to expression.

Performance is

spectacle, a circus of personalities swinging from light trees, dancing on catwalks, balancing on support beams; glittering theatrics, tricks of all kinds, magical doors, illusions for the eye.

Performance is

a demonstration, a public unveiling of one's understanding, unfolding as a qualified question or as a potent proclamation nudging or forcing its way into the ongoing conversation, a conversation controlled by those who know what counts as proof.

Performance is

a tired old friend, telling the same old tales in the same worn clothes, a pathetic figure who wonders why you do not want to listen, why you do not come to the door, why the lights are out.

Performance is

a political act, at times charged with fury like a warring horde, screaming as it rushes into battle, ready to claim its rights and shed its anger; at times blinded by thoughtless thugs with their assumptions of normalcy and decisions of indifference.

Performance is

upon a time, once told, an imaginary moment that goes a tick beyond; a time when time stops counting, when the heart need not beat, when one says, "Actually, never."

Performance is
a corrective, a righting of wrongs, a quick fix found in slick slogans, tied into neat packages and wrapped in ribbon, sealed and stamped for delivery, directed by Don Quixote.

Performance is
a buzzword stretched beyond recognition, blurring genres, a paradigm maker and a paradigm breaker, a theoretical model of human action, a hot ticket for an old revival.

Performance is
an aesthetic encounter, a seductive coalescence that catches you in time, a luscious lure that pulls you in close and pushes you away, over and over, as you lean forward, engaged and giddy, on the top of a sparkle of light.

Performance is
fakery, a masking of the real, a fabrication designed to deceive perpetrated on the gullible, a lie soliciting belief, brazen as a politician or priest.

Performance is
a random guess about human nature, a lucky turn, a spinning wheel where you might get named, an estimate rounded off to the nearest person.

Performance is
holy, a place of worship consecrated for the devoted who gather in its name to listen to the sacred scripts, to join in the hallowed ceremony, to make the spirits rise as the world whirls away.

Performance is
a poem, a poetics of the everyday, counted in syllables and rhythmic patterns, lyric and dramatic, where one ponders the lines and muses the mathematics of it all.

Being a Witness

11

On Looking On

Entering

They knew they would feel out of place unless they had dressed up. Only in those avant-garde theatres is the opposite true. So, they dressed, making themselves slick as a sermon. After fighting traffic and finding parking, they walk among those who are gathering and among those who understand. They fit right in as they look for others whom they know. They linger in the lobby, rubbing their tickets in their hands. They nibble on the memorabilia of past shows and the promise of things still to come. They stand before the publicity shots of the actors, mounted behind glass and smiles. Entering the theatre, they hear the muffled rumble of voices, filled with anticipation. Programs in hand, their bodies move by bodies, in search of their seats. Once found, they settle in like birds ready to nest. They notice who holds the seats beside them. They check their view of the stage, remembering the assurances when they bought their tickets. One says pleased, "He said these would be good seats!" Another says with displeasure, "He said these would be good seats!" They thumb through their programs and note a few details. The energy of the moment pulls them away from print. Seeing that the house is almost full, they wait and share tidbits they have heard about the play. They check their watches. They sense, as the noise of the house swells, that it is about to begin. On cue, they fall silent and together, following the light, they look on.

The Entrance

To get to his seat, Frank had to walk across the front of the stage. The house was almost full. Frank spotted several people he knew in the audience. At first he felt a little self-conscious, but he stopped to chat with someone in the front row, he shook another person's hand, and then he waved to someone else. He sensed the audience was watching him. He started to move toward his seat when the idea struck. Frank did not reflect upon it. He just felt he had to act upon this simple opportunity. Instinct ruled the moment. Frank moved to center stage, looked directly at the audience, and took a long, deep bow. The audience applauded. Some, particularly those who knew Frank, thought the moment was funny; some thought he was foolish. But everyone, even those who disapproved, had to acknowledge that they had never seen a bow with such pure elegance and passion.

Late Arrivals

A flashlight becomes a follow-spot, marking the arrival of late comers. They move in shadows, quickly, hushed, down the aisle before sliding past others into their seats. Most try to ignore them. Some display their displeasure with a simple frown or a shaking of the head. Others twist and turn as they pass so that they never have to stop looking straight ahead. Still others find the late comers' performance the one of greatest interest. Once seated, they are just members of the crowd.

Children

In the theatre, Catherine thought, children should neither be heard nor seen. They have their Disney World and their water parks. They need not bother coming to events they cannot comprehend. They only wiggle their little bottoms until their chairs squeak. They whisper to persons who presumably have their charge but who act as if their wards have as much right to be speaking as the actors. They squeal and squawk when others are clapping. They squirm. They wriggle. They twist. They turn. They kick the people in front of them. They kneel in front of those behind. They play with their hair. They drool on the seats. They drop things on the floor. And after it is all over, they want to hear how well behaved they are and when they might come again.

The adaptation of Lewis Carroll's *Through the Looking-Glass* had been staged well, filled with colorful costumes and performed with wit and charm. Even the set had been built so that at particular moments the actors could walk straight down a set of stairs and interact directly with the children. But perhaps because there were so many young ones in the audience, perhaps because of the stairs, or perhaps because it simply seemed like fun, the children stole the show. Perhaps it should have come as no surprise when the children attempted to sit at the table with Tweedledee and Tweedledum, when they tried to keep Humpty Dumpty from falling from the wall, or when they rushed onstage to gather the playing cards the Queen's soldiers had thrown up in the air.

Being Cast Without Auditioning

Bob felt he was in trouble as soon as he found himself onstage. He had tried to resist, but once he gave his name and the crowd started chanting "We want Bob. We want Bob," he felt he had no choice. He listened to his instructions, knowing that all the comedy from this routine would be at his expense. He was given a plastic sword and crown. He was told that when cued, he was to pull the sword from its sheath, walk forward with sword raised, and then say, "No man can have my daughter's hand unless he is a noble knight." When the finger pointed, he did what he was told to do. Everyone howled. He was told to try again. He did and, again, everyone howled. On the third try, applause. He didn't mind being silly. He didn't mind being laughed at. He did mind, though, not knowing why they laughed.

The chairs were arranged in a semicircle when Jan entered the convention program on collaborative performance work. When she selected a seat slightly off center, she didn't expect that anyone would be performing. As part of the first presentation, however, a woman staged a piece from the point of view of a rapist. The piece starts out with playful teasing but quickly turns aggressive and violent. Jan was selected, without forewarning, as the target of the rapist's interests. The rapist's verbal attack never stopped. It became increasingly intense, hostile, crazed. Jan sat still, motionless, simply focusing on the performer. Her mouth was set into a small, nervous smile. She was onstage. She didn't know what she should do. Her instincts were telling her to strike out, escape. But, having been cast, she remained. She felt like a victim.

Tami's hand would always shoot up when they asked for volunteers. She was ready to be a player. She couldn't understand why some people just wanted to sit back and watch. For her, that was no fun. She wanted to be doing, to be in the thick of things. She had perfected her strategy for getting selected, one that worked just about every time. She would move to the edge of her seat and, if needed, lift herself slightly out of it. Then she would raise her hand higher than anyone else's, put on the cutest smile she could, and repeat, "Me, me, me," until picked.

Confusing Performers and Their Roles

Harriet knew it was just a role that Gary had played. She didn't know, however, that Gary could be so convincing. He was cruel, vicious, vindictive. He relished his nefarious ways. He settled into the role as if he had found a home. Even though Gary never acted that way around Harriet, she couldn't stop seeing that in him. The role hung around him like a poisonous vapor. She couldn't accept that he could act in such a manner, that he could utter such words, that he could have such a capacity.

Tracy had seen Sam play the leading man many times. He had all the right attributes: handsome and virile, coupled with a boyish charm. He knew just what to say. When she met him, she found him handsome and virile, coupled with a boyish charm. He knew just what to say.

Named from the Stage

Paula felt she had little choice but to pretend she was enjoying the show when she was named in the annual Christmas theatre follies put on by the undergraduate theatre majors. She knew that they were informed about her life, even her relationship with Katherine. In fact, she often used details from her own experiences as examples when she was teaching. She felt that personal experiences are a rich resource for the actor. She never tried to hide anything about her life from her students. But when she saw Katherine and herself being portrayed onstage by two men in drag who were barking orders at each other like drill sergeants, she felt betrayed. She wanted to change everything. She wanted to cast the scene with women who understood, to change the tone, to silence the laughter.

The only condition Mariangela gave when asked if she would mind if he told their story onstage was that he use their names. She knew that the tale he wanted to tell might not present her in the best light. But she argued that to stop the telling would be to claim possession of what she did not own and to change their names would be in some way to disown the experience, an experience in which she had invested considerable time over the last few years. Besides, she continued, those in the audience who mattered to her knew their story and would recognize it even if their names were changed, and those in the audience she didn't know wouldn't be able to connect the names with the people. She was surprised following the performance by the number of people who wanted to know how she felt about having intimate details from her life put onstage. After the third inquiry, she settled into a short answer that captured, when given the right inflection, her conflicting feelings: "It's just one story."

"Imagine being in a relationship with him," Liz said to her friend as they left a performance of Spalding Gray's *Monster in a Box*. "Poor Renee," she went on. "Just think about living with someone who turns everything you do together into a performance piece. I'd be afraid to do anything. I mean, we might be making love and what he'd be thinking is how this is material for his next monologue. Why does he want to tell about these things anyway? Poor Renee. I can't believe she puts up with it."

Being Accused

The finger was pointing at them. The message was clear: They had not done enough; they were part of the problem. The phrase "we are responsible" hung in the air. Some accepted the charge like an overdue bill. Others resisted, refusing to see themselves in the "we." Believing themselves falsely accused, they sat there angrily, denying any accountability, smug as self-righteous Republicans.

Alex and Barbara were moved. Seeing the suffering, they felt guilty. They had known there were problems, but it was quite another thing to hear about them in detail, to watch them staged, to witness such horrors. They decided they had to do something. On the spot, they wrote out a check for one hundred dollars and then, feeling better, left the theatre for a café au lait.

Noticing Others in the House

Clara's raucous laugh, booming out over that of all others, came frequently and from deep within. Everyone would look. They were alarmed. What they heard was a braying guffaw, a noise one might associate with a wild beast that had just killed its prey. The coarse burst would punch its way into existence like a boisterous pugilist taking on all challengers. The bellowing clamor would rattle the rafters and ravage the room. The vociferous sound would persevere like an incorrigible child intent on getting onstage.

At first, Ann didn't mind. She was sure that they would stop. But they continued, quietly, but loud enough to be distracting. Putting on her disapproving face, she turned and gave them a look. They didn't stop. She tolerated the noise for a couple of minutes more before she turned again. "Please," she said, "I'm trying to listen." "Sorry," he quipped, "we'll try to talk a little louder."

It was the story of their engagement, the story of their love, that made Chris cry. He was sitting in the center of the house, and she was speaking from the stage directly to him. As he listened to the details, tears rushed down his cheeks. He wanted to stand and announce his love for her. He leaned forward to be nearer to her. He threw her a kiss. He cried. Everyone could see the connection between them. Everyone could see the love they shared. It was sweet and sentimental and, somehow, alright.

Black and White

Terry couldn't believe how they would behave. No matter what was going on, they would punctuate what the actors said with their "uh huh's" and their "that's right's." They just felt free to call out at anytime. When they laughed, they would nearly fall from their seats. When they cried, they would wail. They would come in late and would leave early if they didn't like what was going on. Terry explained it all when she remembered that they hadn't had all the opportunities she has had and that they hadn't been taught how to act. It was as clear to her as black and white.

Tamara couldn't believe how they would just sit there, stiff and still. They were like robots programmed to respond together, all with the same look, laugh, and clap. Their bodies were mechanical, tight as a spring, so machinelike she imagined that someone might be controlling them, perhaps some crazed computer whiz who had created millions of white people, automatons who were designed to like musicals and who were wired to take over the earth. The thought made her shiver.

Expectations

It had everything going for it—the hottest new playwright, a well-seasoned, Tony Award-winning director, and a top-notch cast, including a big-time Hollywood star in the leading role. Robert got his seat months in advance. He told everyone in the office about going. On the night he was to attend, he sang as he dressed. He left the house early, giving himself time to spare. He imagined that this show would stay with him forever. He just knew it would be wonderful. It wasn't.

Ellen found herself laughing. She had told Brian that she didn't want to go, that she didn't much like live theatre. He had insisted, and simply to keep peace, she relented. She remembered the Shakespeare show she had to see for her English class. She could barely understand the actors, and the play seemed to drag on forever. She thought about the times her parents brought her to the summer musicals. They just seemed silly to her—people singing to one another as if it were perfectly natural and singing songs that only people like her parents could enjoy. She preferred films. So, when she found herself laughing, she wondered if Brian would say, "I told you so."

Faking Interest

As the adjudicator, Dr. Jenkins knew that she was being watched, that people would read meaning into how she behaved while viewing the show. It had started out well enough, but the play had just too much exposition and had characters it was difficult to care about. The quality of performance was adequate but nothing remarkable. The set was well done. It was quite functional and struck the right tone and mood, but it couldn't sustain interest. Dr. Jenkins tried to pay attention but became increasingly aware of her own performance—the pleasant smile she placed on her face, the erect posture she took on to keep her body in place, the occasional slight nodding of the head she employed to signal her engagement. She thought she was doing a wonderful job. She was surprised after making some comments to the cast when someone said, "Gee, after watching you during the show, I thought you hated it."

Tim wanted Shea to sit next to him on his opening night. It had become a tradition over the years, a tradition Shea came to resent. Shea believed Tim was a first-rate director. He loved Tim's work, always had, and could not imagine not liking something Tim had done. He just didn't like sitting next to Tim during one of Tim's shows. Tim seemed to be waiting for his every response, noting when he laughed, when he turned his head, when he rubbed his nose. Shea wanted to watch without being watched. He wanted to be taken off Tim's stage. He wanted to be free of the responsibility.

Intermission

Time to make an assessment, to look back and to speculate about what is to come. Time, if needed, to catch your breath. Time, if needed, to rub the sleep from your eyes. Time to get something to drink and to attend to private matters. Time to see what others are thinking, what others are whispering. Time to decide if you want to continue.

With Permission to Gaze

Theatre is about looking, but this felt different to Jake. There they were right before him: six actors with physical disabilities, three in wheelchairs, one with Canadian crutches, three with missing parts. They were talking about what it means to be a person with a disability and were using their own particular disabilities for illustrative purposes. Jake stared even as he remembered from his boyhood days his parents' corrective: "It's not nice to stare." He felt confused, guilty. He could not stop looking. He pretended that what he was seeing was familiar, ordinary, unremarkable. But his eyes would return to the fingers coming from the shoulder, the tiny arms and legs from the adult trunk, the leg in a twisted jerk struggling to follow. He heard their message: See the person, not the disability. He had to admit that he could not.

Harry isn't against nudity. In fact, he rather likes it, just not onstage. Perhaps it is because he likes viewing nude bodies that he doesn't want it onstage. He finds it distracting, even when it is central to the play. When Harry is faced with nudity, he can't help thinking about how the nude scene was negotiated, how the actor stripped that first night in rehearsal. He can't help wondering how the actor feels about being nude onstage. He can't help speculating about the actor's reaction to the presence of others in the audience—strangers, parents, friends. He can't help wanting to go onstage and wrap the actor in his coat. He can't help feeling adolescent. So, when Harry had a front-row seat in a small intimate theatre that was staging *Equus* and when Harry, sharing Alan's perspective, saw Jill strip and lay, legs spread, directly in front of him, he did not keep his mind on the play.

Karen's mastectomy occurred about a month before she found herself sitting in a theatre listening to personal narratives about cancer. She saw herself in their stories: the difficulties in dealing with loved ones, the aloof medical establishment, the body as the residence of the enemy, the fear. She saw too her frail body onstage, a body without color, without hair. She appreciated the carefully crafted tales that described without exaggeration, that used humor without lessening, that unfolded without pity. She noticed a woman in the audience who was slightly rocking in her seat, tears running down her clean, open face, stunned by the horror and pain of it all. Karen, remembering who is licensed to cry, knew that woman did not have cancer.

Kevin said it didn't really matter to him if someone was gay. He said that even though he was straight, he had several gay friends. He said sexual preference was just that, a preference. Kevin was proud to be a good liberal. Kevin was so proud to be a good liberal that he went to see David Dillon's comedy *Party*, the play about seven gay men who entertain themselves by participating in a strip version of truth or dare. As Kevin watched, he wondered if everyone in the cast was gay or if anyone was just acting. He pondered. He wanted to know if he could tell. He examined them, noting their gestures, the way they walked, the sound of their voices. Kevin just felt more secure when he knew.

Laughing over Objections

Everyone in the audience was laughing. Jim was laughing too, but he thought he shouldn't be. He felt that humor at the expense of others just isn't funny. His laughter was weak, hollow, uncertain. He wondered if he was being, perhaps, too rigid, too caught up in political correctness.

After all, he could see why everyone was laughing. This was funny if you didn't think about who might be hurt by it. Besides, they should be able to laugh at themselves. People take themselves too seriously. Jim couldn't quite convince himself of these arguments. He still felt uneasy when what happened onstage was so funny, he just couldn't contain himself.

When It's Awful

Their heads are most telling. Some are resting in hands; some are turned down; some are eyeing the door. Bodies twist and turn in their seats. Arms rest in front of chests. Legs cross, back and forth, from left to right, right to left. Fingers tap, pick lint, play with themselves. Hands rub faces. It is a time to think about those sitting around them: their clothes, their partners, their lives. It is a time to think about tomorrow. Someone may nod off. Someone may search a purse or a coat pocket for a mint. Someone may whisper. Someone may escape. Someone may catch another's eye so that, together, their eyes may roll. They are prisoners, caught by their own unfulfilled desires, obeying prison rules but refusing to eat the slop put before them.

When It's Wonderful

They breathe together. They laugh, cry, groan together. They are still, titling forward, heads cocked. Their bodies disappear. They listen. They are ready, anticipating, hungry for more. Together, they sense each other's presence. They are being served as a group, put together at a round table. They toast the banquet before them. It sticks to their ribs. Their bodies reappear, giddy as peeled grapes. They say to one another as they pull closer to the table, "Isn't this wonderful!" Their eyes are wide as saucers. Their bodies disappear as if sliding into a good stew.

Trying to Stay Awake

Immediately after the lights went down, Ralph was in trouble. He had been up much of the night before, finishing a report, and then had put in a long day at the office. Coming to the play was his treat to himself for getting everything done. It took about fifteen minutes for it to happen. First, he noticed the glare, almost a haze, separating the audience and the actors. It was as if someone had placed a soft curtain across the front of the stage. He felt secure and anonymous. Second, the actors were going on about this and that, problems he had heard about most of his life. He didn't really care how they worked through their plight. Third, his eyes grew heavy and his head dropped. Startled and embarrassed, he tried to shake himself awake. It worked for about five minutes. Then he felt his wife's nudge. He tried to listen again but was soon gone. He awoke to applause, and for a slight instance, he thought everyone was acknowledging his subtle, yet committed, snooze.

Critics

Some are guides, pointing out the difficult terrain and the splendors to behold. Some are historians, remembering the old and recording the new. Some are authorities, pronouncing verdicts as they sharpen the ax. Some are indiscriminate, promiscuous lovers, embracing all. Some are reporters who describe without ever telling how they might feel. Some are wits who look more often to their readers than to the stage. Some are financial consultants, eyeing the stock of the winners and losers and advising where to invest. Some are diplomats, forming coalitions, building bridges, and apologizing when needed. Some are scholars, theorizing performance and performing theory.

Exiting Early

Alan whispered to Michele, "Do you want to get out of here?" He wasn't sure how she would respond. He only knew that he couldn't take much more of this. All this preaching was just too much. He preferred shows that made you think, engaged you with ideas. But moral platitudes, whether he is sympathetic to the cause or not, make for poor theatre. He wanted to escape. Michele nodded that she was ready. She wanted to slip out quietly, unnoticed. She had hoped to find the right moment to leave, perhaps between scenes, but Alan, after seeing her nod, was out of his seat, excusing himself down the row. She followed, embarrassed, glancing at the stage as she left. Outside, Alan was loud and loquacious, mocking the actors and ridiculing the play. He was relieved and finally enjoying himself. Michele laughed, shushing him, feeling free as a kid skipping school.

Applause

Some is perfunctory, simply marking the end and carrying a note of disappointment. Some is cautious, caught in indecision. Some is solid, steady, sealed against complaint. Some is firm as a handshake, a recognition of good faith. Some is as delicate as a hundred hands joining in a circle. Some is profuse, rushing out like warriors, determined to be heard. Some is generous, offered as a return gift, wrapped forever.

Standing Ovations

Emily had always felt that to leap from one's seat following a performance somehow demonstrated a lack of sophistication. When she elected to stand, it was only after a number of other people had. And she would do it slowly, ensuring that no one might mistake her praise as complete. Once up, she performed her reservations in the rhythm of her applause. Ken, on the other hand, was quick to stand. He didn't mind it if he was the only one. It was like leaping into an imaginary world before it would fade. He would stand there, clapping loudly, to look again at the actors, marveling at their powers and telling them of his pleasure. He would stand there, waiting through the curtain's blink, wanting it never to end. He would stand there, unashamed.

Exiting

When the applause stops, they leave. Gathering their things, they file out, slowly, more quietly than they came. They want to talk, but they are thinking, processing, still searching for what they want to say. Bunched together, they move, hands at their sides, in half steps up the aisles. They look around, knowing that they must wait before they can speak freely. They remember where they parked the car and consider going for dessert and coffee. Their clothes are wrinkled. They twist and roll their programs. They hear someone say, "Wasn't it wonderful?" They glance around, trying to spot the person who would offer such a public assessment. They edge forward. They keep the people they came with in sight. The ends of the aisles open like mouths yawning. They spill out into their private lives, in groups of two, three, or four, looking to each other and wondering what might be said.

Going Backstage

Steven hated the tradition of going backstage. What could one really say? He toyed with the idea of declaring exactly what he thought: "You should never go onstage again." "Aren't you tired of using the same tricks with every role you get?" "You missed the point of the play." The whimsy passed when he saw their faces, eager for a comforting stroke. He remembered his own feelings of vulnerability at such times. So instead, he offered smiles and hugs and words of praise. At times he was sincere, other times not. For those he could not praise, he would exclaim, "What interesting work!" or, "My! That was something."

Unwinding

Certain things have to get put on the table. They just can't be held back. Others percolate until they are ready to be served. Some simmer, perhaps never to come out. Others are free of spice, bland as white bread. Some need a steak knife to cut through; for others, a butter knife will do. Some are crisp as lettuce, some as cruel as cabbage. Others are sweet; some are sour. Others get put in the stew. Some are left over. Some become tomorrow's soup.

Consequences

They had been at each other for over an hour, when Rebecca thought of the play they had seen together a few years ago. It was about the emptiness a woman had in her marriage. She felt that nothing mattered, not her husband nor her children. At the end of the play, the woman, feeling trapped in a relationship she could not abide, commits suicide. Remembering that moment, Rebecca decided to leave him.

It was a familiar story. Henry had heard it all before. The next day when asked what he had seen, he couldn't remember.

During the AIDS benefit, Mark made his commitment. He had decided while he was listening to the performers tell the stories of those with AIDS and of those who lost someone they loved to AIDS. He needed to do something with his tears, with his anger. He needed to take some action. For the last three years now, Mark has volunteered ten hours a week in hospice care.

"I thought you said you hated it," Helen said. "Yes, I did," Linda answered, "but it won't leave me alone. I can't get it out of my mind."

12

Doing the New York Scene

It is after 6:00 by the time I check into the Gramercy Park Hotel. Without unpacking, I head straight for the TKTS booth in Duffy Square. Not much is up. I decide to gamble on Christopher Kyle's *The Monogamist* at Playwrights Horizons. It's a safe gamble, since something interesting is always there. Twenty dollars, a slice of pizza, and a wrong turn on 42nd Street (how could I get turned around?) later, I'm sitting in the theatre watching images, primarily dealing with sexuality. The play is about an avant-garde poet who faces a midlife crisis after finding his wife, a Princeton professor, in bed with one of her students. There are some clever lines and a few moments that are genuinely funny, but in the end, the play offers up five characters you don't trust or like. Completing the cast are the self-absorbed idiotic poet, the adulterous professor who cannot maintain a conversation without exploding, two brainless twenty-something kids, and an over-the-top literary critic who mashes feminist thought into her own perverse interests. These are people you could have done without meeting. During the intermission, I chat with the woman seated next to me. She is a creative-writing student at Columbia University, a charming person whose laughter is deep, warm, and free.

Leaving the theatre, I start to walk. I go only a short way before seeing a fight about a half a block away. That is theatre I don't want to witness. I turn, hail a cab, and return to the hotel. Ready for coffee the next morning, I leave the Gramercy. Without deciding to do so, I find myself strolling, coffee in hand. I make it to Union Square. I stare at the sellers of fruits, vegetables, breads, and flowers and wonder about their lives—where they grow their produce, what hassles they must confront coming into the city, how they could make enough money to make it worthwhile. During my reflections, a Dalmatian pees by the park bench I'm sitting on, and I hear its owner say, "Don't do that on that man." I smile, signaling that I was out of harm's way.

In line at Duffy Square, I confuse two titles: Harold Pinter's *Moonlight*, the story of a terminally ill man and his family, with Bill Irwin and David Shiner's *Fool Moon*, the show of the vaudevillian mimes that gets their laughs by playing off the audience. I picked the wrong one. We witness Irwin and Shiner do such bits as literally climbing over the audience to find a seat; pulling audience members from their seats and putting them onstage in melodrama scenes; and taking pratfall after pratfall as they try on audience members' clothes, snap photographs with an audience member's camera, and swipe audience members' belongings. Of course, this street theatre on Broadway is all in good fun. Everyone gets applause for being such good sports. Everything is returned to order. Of course, no real harm is done. No one is really in harm's way.

Having bought a copy of the *Village Voice* and *Time Out*, I read in Washington Square about theatre possibilities. I hear a man yell, "Don't come near me. I'm a menace to society." He laughs as people heed his advice. I move on to the NYU campus: The young, with backpacks slung over their shoulders, hurry on, wise as the tough streets they follow. I hit Bleecker Street, one of my favorites to meander. A T-shirt in the window of a small shop displays the words "Tourists Go Home." I follow the Avenue of the Americas into the Soho art district, but I'm too early for any of the galleries to be open. I hit Spring Street and remember reading that Poets House is located there. I use the Spring Street Book Store to get the exact address. I locate it and find myself, after several hours, still browsing. With limited time, I am unwilling to give up an evening of theatre for an evening of poets reading, despite seeing in the "Poetry Calendar" many upcoming poetry events that I think I would enjoy.

Heading back to Duffy Square, I decide I have time to walk. I pass merchants leaning on door frames, waiting for customers to come and the day to end. I pass New Yorkers, dressed smooth as minted breath, who move as if getting where they are going matters. I pass those huddled in doorways, wrapped in plastic and soiled blankets, sleeping, with no place to go. I arrive, and after an hour wait, pay thirty-two fifty for a ticket to *The Heiress*. Loosely based on the Henry James novel *Washington Square*, the play is a study of a stern and seemingly protective father's influence on a shy heiress when a gold-digging suitor appears. At the intermission, the woman sitting next to me asks, "Who do you think the villain is?" I say, saying too much, "Everyone, the father who keeps telling her how she doesn't measure up to her mother, the aunt who sends the same message, and, of course, her suitor who wants her money." "I think it's just the father," she says. At the end of the play, she asks again, "Who do you think the villain is?" I start to answer, but she insists again: "It's the father. It's the father." We part, and I wonder why that assessment is so important to her. I'd rather celebrate the heiress's sad and poignant triumph as she turns her suitor away in the final scene.

The next morning I'm off to explore the East Village. I want to walk the Alphabet City—Avenues A, B, C, D in search of Galway Kinnell's poem, "The Avenue Bearing the Initial of Christ into the New World."

But his poem is not there. There is no "pcheek pcheek" of birds crying, nor the vibrating voices of Israel, Africa, Puerto Rico, China, France, and the Caribbean, nor the struggle of people surviving. These streets are silent, still, empty, bearing the exhaustion of years. These streets have no songs, not ones of shattered glass, nor ones of broken buildings, nor ones of staring eyes. Its note is dull as a forgotten dream. Depressed, I catch a cab for a matinee of *Les Miserables*. Nothing can help you forget like believing your heart is in the right place.

Recharged, I fall back into line at the TKTS booth. I meet Vinny, an ex-priest, lawyer, and CEO of a new company selling electric cars. When we reach the board, Vinny says he hates seeing shows alone and asks if I'd like to join him. I recommend Bob Becker's *Defending the Caveman*, the one-man comedy show on the differences between the sexes, coding, perhaps too subtly, my own predilections. We have a few hours before the show, and Vinny suggests we get something to eat. I agree. "Why don't we go back to my hotel first so I can change. It's just a few block away," Vinny says. I follow, wondering if I'm being picked up and wondering if I'm being a rube in the big city. "You know, I travel a lot, and it gets lonely," Vinny continues. "I'm glad you decided to join me." When we arrive at the hotel, I say, "I have to make a phone call, so I'll just wait for you down here." Vinny nods and then adds, "I'm in Room 1617 if you want to come up." I don't. Five minutes later, we are off to dinner. He is charming. He talks about the problems of a celibate priesthood and how his home became a halfway house for priests who decided to return to secular life. He offers his views on the decline of American cities, views filled with details from his work during the Detroit riots. He mentions that his wife recently died. We chat until curtain time, discovering that we share many of the same beliefs. "Being a bleeding heart liberal like I am," I say, "how do you justify paying Broadway ticket prices?" "Balance," he answers. Sitting next to Vinny during *Defending the Caveman*, I watch him laughing and feel embarrassed about needing to defend my cave.

The next day I'm walking, listening: Japanese, French, Spanish, Russian, Hindi, and others I can't identify. Fragments of conversations enter me: "Maria, wait." "There's a hundred dollar plate dinner." "Fuck that shit." "Oh my god, I fell asleep in that. Did you like it?" "Last night I dreamed about a lizard. It's weird. The last time you were sick, I dreamed about a lizard." For a moment, I live their lives. A pigeon pecks along the steps of the New York Public Library. Its green and purple breast is balanced by its four fingered claws. Finding its way among the young students who eat their lunch in the midday sun, its head bobs in search of crumbs. A street performer, telling bad jokes, can't get the attention of the reading and eating crowd.

That night I see Nicky Silver's *The Food Chain*. It strikes me as a play in the Neil Simon *Barefoot in the Park* genre, tight and contrived. The play features silly people and simple stereotypes: a dithery poet who acts as if she is being profound by titling her poems "Untitled" followed by a number; a Jewish mother who works a crisis hot line but never listens; an obese gay man who never stops eating; a gay male model who is fixated on his own beauty; and the object of the poet's and the model's desire, a tall dark man who never speaks. The directing and acting is so forced it becomes painful to watch. Despite the promise of the reviews, for me there is no nourishment, nothing much even to nibble on.

Missing my family, I call wanting to hear the details of their lives. I learn that our close friends have decided to divorce. Later, I stand in the World Trade Center Plaza, dizzy, looking at the two towers thrust into the sky. Giants see themselves in these glass mirrors. I enter Tower II to buy tickets for Jean Cocteau's *Indiscretions*. Still later, I read the list of tenants in the Empire State Building: Both Jockey International and Fruit of the Loom operate from King Kong's hangout. With his shy, questioning look, he was the king of pickup artists. Much later, I am engrossed in *Indiscretions*, the dark comedy about a possessive, perhaps incestuous, mother's relationship to her son. The fine performance work of Kathleen Turner, Dana Ivey, and Roger Rees is eclipsed, though, by Jude Law, not with his full frontal nudity as *Time Out* suggests but with his raw, charismatic energy. On 42nd Street, the sex shops offer promises they cannot keep.

Exploring Chelsea the next day, I misread my *Fodor's 96: New York City* guidebook. I take an address for an avenue. Instead of discovering Chelsea's Book Row, I find car repair shops, metal works, and lumberyards. My pace quickens as I try to read the markings of gangs sprayed on the beaten buildings. I do not know this language. I am not on my own turf. I do not know how to read. I am ready, ticket in hand, to return to my territory, The Booth Theatre, to see *Having Our Say*, the wonderful adaptation of the autobiography of the two over-one-hundred-year-old Delaney sisters. They tell of the joys and sadnesses they've had during their one hundred years as well as the racial injustices they've had to confront as black Americans. Their tale is inspirational to all of us middle-class, Broadway-theatre-going, white and black audience members who believe that with just hard work and perseverance, anyone can have the American dream. Charged by the power of the performance, I decide to walk back to my hotel. Late at night, following Broadway from 45th to 21st, the streets are empty, except for occasional figures in dark shadows. The gangs begin to speak to me again in a language I do not know. I move quickly, afraid of the dark. I am a racist.

Daylight and, again, I'm walking. I pass massive apartment complexes, the brown hives where the worker bees live. Busily, they push on, believing that they must. I, an amateur entomologist, examine them closely and marvel at their intricate work. I have come to take their honey, to feed off their labors. I want to join the swarm, unnoticed, buzzing along, stinger ready, in search of nectar. I want to fly along, weaving in and out, curving here and there, pausing for a moment just to get my bearings. But I will leave the workers undisturbed, unmarked, untroubled by my presence. I will leave them still working.

The Guggenheim Museum is exhibiting the work of Claes Oldenburg, the artist who recreates, often in grand scale, everyday inanimate objects. From his "Soft Toilet" to his forty-five-foot-high sculpture, "Clothespin," he makes us see, perhaps for the first time, what is always around us. Through the use of scale, color, and humor, Oldenburg makes us remember our own bodies moving through the world. A man, moving off the gentle spiral presenting Oldenburg's work, enters the space that houses some of the Guggenheim's permanent collection. He announces to his wife, "Now, this is more like it!" Later, he decides he need not bother to see more than the first few photographs of the Joel-Peter Witkins exhibit. "Who wants to see a woman with a penis?" he asks. I leave the Guggenheim remembering an Oldenburg quote: "I make my work out of my everyday experiences, which I find as perplexing and extraordinary as can be."

The United States Post Office on 8th Avenue, between 33rd and 34th, is a structure that fills an entire block. On its facade, supported by twenty columns, is the mail carriers' creed: "Neither snow, nor rain, nor heat, nor gloom of night stays these couriers from the swift completion of their appointed rounds." Inside this formidable building, a small card containing five dollars and birthday wishes to a grandchild sits for months in the corner on the floor. Later, I poke my nose into a gallery, only long enough to see that it is featuring a photographic remembrance of Elvis Presley. I move on to the Soho Guggenheim Museum to see Dieter Appelt's photographic display. His violent, disturbing images will not leave me. "Pitigliano" is a close-up black and white series showing two fingers being shoved into a women's eyes. "Canto II" is also a close-up black and white series of a thumb, nail turned inward, pushing into the side of a mouth, set against a day-old beard. It takes a moment to realize what one is seeing. It takes a moment to realize what one can see. I want more distance, more color. I want to lose the images. I cannot.

Patty Chang's one-woman show, "At A Loss," staged at P.S. 122 gives me images too, images that are stronger than her language, images that override the story she wants to tell. In scene one, she enters, tied to a chair with a wire gag in her mouth, struggling to speak. In scene two, she appears on toe for an extended period of time, wobbling back and forth across the stage, as if trying to keep her balance. In scene three, she is blindfolded, lifts her full hoop skirt, and proceeds to soap and shave her pubic hair. In the final scene, she remains blindfolded. She puts on two false breasts, cantaloupes, pulls a knife from between them and slices one open. With a saucer on her head for the seeds, she eats the cantaloupe hollow with a spoon, as she finishes her monologue. Through her images, we see the struggle of women to speak freely and to maintain their balance as they confront various discursive fields. We watch the lure of and abhorrence to objectifying eyes. We remember that continuing to participate in the patriarchal hegemony is a destructive act of self-consumption. But we forget Patty Chang in the wake of her theorizing. We do not see the Patty Chang for whom all this matters. And when she returns to stage to greet her friends after the show is over, her warmth, hidden before, burst forth from her body to tell of another Patty Chang, the one who can find her way around her images in order to live.

Piet Mondrian (1872–1944), whose retrospective is showing at The Museum of Modern Art, also speaks a language of the abstract. He escapes the limits of representation in the name of the line, a pure structure known as "neoplasticism." His lines move beyond the canvas, beyond himself. But for me, a critic without schooling, his lines move only to theory and to the power of institutional placement. But I respond to his early work, the disturbing Van Gogh surrealism of "Red Tree," the seductive Picasso cubism of "Gray Tree," and the realism of his charcoal drawing "Self-Portrait: Eyes." Those eyes hold you in place, insist that you linger, wonder. And I respond to his final paintings, when life returns with its jazz rhythms and bright colors in a "Broadway Boogie Woogie."

Carol Channing, at seventy-four, adds each night to her over forty-five hundred performances of *Hello, Dolly!* in her own Broadway boogie woogie. No longer able to dance or sing as well as she once did, she carries such charm for her audiences that they don't seem to care. They leap to their feet in wild applause as she enters, as she sings their favorite songs, and as the curtain comes down. Tears mark their faces. And when this cultural icon elects to grace the audience with her curtain speech about the worldwide tour of *Dolly*, they swoon. And, of course, knowing it will happen before she says it, this woman of the stage speaks as if confused why everyone is still standing there: "You dear people, you just don't seem to be leaving."

On the corner of Mercer and 4th in front of the Courant Institute of Mathematical Sciences, I try to understand the arithmetic of it all. As I sit I startle two women who gather their packages. A professor walks by, yawning. A woman studies her head shots and smiles. A man moves with his poodle; another with his Doberman. A mother pushes her child in a stroller, feeding her cookies. A woman, sporting a cowboy hat, strides down the street like a sheriff. Without comment, a woman wearing an NYU sweatshirt places a half-eaten dollar seventy-nine bag of Frito-Lay potato chips beside a man of the streets. Under the ginkgo tree, that tree of fingers cresting in a cross, he pulls an orange drink from his coat pocket and has dinner. He pushes his blue hood from his bald head, turns the chip bag inside out, and feeds the sparrows.

Images matter. I meet some friends for dinner, before the Halloween parade in the Village: Craig, a gay performance artist, and Lisa and Denise, two lesbian scholars who have been together for years. Without costumes, we appear as two lovely heterosexual couples, chatting our way down the street. We line up, three deep, to watch those in the parade pass. There are the familiar figures of Halloween: ghosts, werewolves, and Franken-steins. There are the unexpected: Richard Nixon, a toilet with plunger, and a fire hydrant. There are the gender benders: women as men, the half-men half-women, and the men in drag. The crowd in front of us begins to tease the police officer standing nearby. They summon men in drag to flirt with him, to drape their arms over his shoulder, to say sweet noth-ings in his ear. Embarrassed and uncomfortable, he smiles throughout, letting it happen with good humor. When the parade ends, Lisa thanks him for showing respect for the gay and lesbian community.

Images matter for The Ridiculous Theatrical Company in their pre-sentation of *Murder at Minsing Manor: A Nancy Boys Mystery*. In this gay send-up of Nancy Drew and the Hardy Boys series, two boys (played by women) go sleuthing when a horror show host is impaled inside an iron maiden. Images slide around: The cross-dressed boys, who engage in mutual masturbation while one reads from *Playboy* and the other from a muscle man magazine; Everett Quinton, the artistic director of the Ri-diculous, as the witty Glory, a character he describes as "W. C. Fields thinking he's Mae West"; Kyle Kennedy as Father Pat, whose fondness for young boys drives his actions and keeps his hands busy; and many others. But these images come without an attitude, without a stance. They invite destructive readings, interpretations at variance with the interests of the Ridiculous. The exception comes with the show's final moment. The Hardy Boys separate, one to join the heterosexual world of bullies who prove they aren't gay by forcing a guy who called them queer to have oral sex with them and the other, isolated by a single stage light, ready to enter the gay world of characters who offer few, if any, appealing scripts to follow.

Reality blurs in the proliferation of images. Nothing holds still, not even for that institution of institutions, The Metropolitan Museum of Art in its "Goya and the Spirit of Enlightenment" exhibition. The final paint-ings, placed side by side, are both entitled "Majas on a Balcony." One, we are assured, is a genuine Goya; the other, belonging to the Museum, we are told may be a Goya or the work of an adroit copyist. Both show two women seated, elegantly dressed, with two dark male figures stand-ing close behind. The Metropolitan's painting, though, is not an exact copy. The women are not curious and questioning, heads tilting into one another, engaged in intimate talk. The figures in the background are not dark and frightened by the women's thinking. The Metropolitan painting turns the angle of the women's heads so that they gaze off away from each other, vacuous, and lit from behind like holy virgins, protected by the overseeing men. I cannot say which is the true Goya, but I know which is genuine, which is enlightened, which is in keeping with his own self-portrait, which could explain his own deep frown.

And what does one do with such realities, from the *Patti LuPone on Broadway* show, with its glitter and pure and powerful music, to Tom Courtenay as Venichka Yerofeev in *Moscow Stations*, the surreal monologue of a disillusioned, alcoholic intellectual? What does one do with the three one-act plays, staged under the title *Death Defying Acts*—with David Mamet's *An Interview*, a play whose existential promise is reduced to a one-line joke about lawyers; Woody Allen's family tragedy turned into the farce *Central Park West*; or Elaine May's *Hotline*, a show that renders suicide as comedy? What does one do to justify spending over five-hundred dollars on museum and theatre tickets? Is it a question of balance or of necessity? What can one do but look, never stop looking, never stop seeing? I gaze, wondering, figuring, demanding. I am only here to witness, to be witnessed, and to bear witness. I am here in the world, fragile as the moment before it all begins.

In the New York Public Library Reading Room, a man reads from a torn paperback entitled *Diana, Her Dark Life*. With a worn Hawaiian brochure, stuffed with wrinkled papers, and the *Essentials of Internal Medicine* surrounding him, he stops to count his money. He makes stacks of tens, twenties, and fifties, looks around, and quickly puts it away. He examines a clipped ad for the film *The Scarlet Letter*, gathers his things, and leaves. Across the table, she, with five sharp red pencils, is working on a manuscript, pages 101 to 141. She circles, underlines, and draws looping arrows. She writes notes on yellow tabs. With a dictionary on her lap, she moves among pages like a desperate prayer. Behind her, another man writes. His fingers fly across the keyboard of his Portege Laptop. Silently mouthing words, he cannot type quickly enough, cannot get it down. He stops abruptly, leans back, sighs, and shuts down. I sit, under the gaze of the golden figures set into the ceiling, with a single sheet of lined paper I've pulled from my pocket, ready, surveying the scene and scribbling some words, in a library where no one sleeps.

13

The *DEF Comedy Jam,*
bell hooks, and Me

Unliess otherwise noted, all quotes in this chapter are from four episodes of the Russell Simmons' DEF Comedy Jam, *dir. Stan Lathan, HBO Time Warner Entertainment, 1994–95.*

In white supremacist capitalist patriarchy, I am flipping channels late on a Saturday night. I stop to listen when I see a stand-up comic. I'm pulled in. I'm curious, surprised, confused. This is not a usual comedy show—all the comics are black, the audience is black, the master of ceremonies, Joe Tory, is black. It's called the *Russell Simmons' DEF Comedy Jam.* I look with the anthropologist gaze, wondering what this is, what this could mean. So I collect episodes, ten to be exact, and I transcribe them, study them for clues.

Talk to me bell. Help me make sense of what I'm hearing, what I'm seeing. Help me understand why I feel as if I'm eavesdropping, listening to talk that I'm not suppose to hear. Help me figure out why I want to figure this out.

> hooks: "Often when black subjects give expression to multiple aspects of our identity, which emerge from a different location, we may be seen by white others as 'spectacle.'" (*Yearning* 22)

In white supremacist capitalist patriarchy, I want to enter this spectacle without a colonizing gaze. My desire is to interrogate, to disrupt my easy assumptions, to dismantle my racist views. I want to end by saying, "I am not a racist." I want to believe what I am saying. But I look and look, pulled in by difference, pulled in by the strangeness, pulled in by the Other.

> hooks: "To begin, what does it mean when primarily white men and women are producing the discourse around Otherness?" (*Yearning* 53)

135

But I cannot refuse to speak because I am privileged to do so. I cannot turn away from dialogue. I cannot close myself off from the other.

> hooks: "Often this speech about 'Other' annihilates, erases: 'No need to hear your voice when I can talk about you better than you can speak about yourself. No need to hear your voice. Only tell me about your pain. I want to know your story. And then I will tell it back to you in a new way. Tell it back to you in such a way that it has become mine, my own. Re-writing you, I write myself anew. I am still author, authority. I am still the colonizer, the speaking subject, and you are now the center of my talk.'" (*Yearning* 151–52)

I will listen. I want to hear the African-American voices. I will claim no authority. I do not know what it means to be DEF, to be cool. I will place those who are talking behind my back in front of me. I will listen even when I am named.

White Folks

In white supremacist capitalist patriarchy, I hear my name. I am offensive, pernicious, laughable. I am ridiculed and mocked by those I have oppressed. I am named how I expect to be. Yet, more is in the naming than I realized. Joe Tory spots two white faces in the audience and he jokes, "If y'all comfortable, I ain't going to fuck with you. I mean, fuck, y'all crazy. I don't fuck with white people. Crazy. Y'all some crazy motherfuckers." In my mind, I too think that they are crazy—how could they get seats down front, within easy view of the comics on the thrust stage? How could they laugh at the jokes without feeling self-conscious? How could they go to such an event and feel safe? They are crazy for having placed their bodies on the wrong side of the tracks, in the wrong neighborhood, with the wrong people. Weren't they afraid?

> hooks: "Today many white people who see themselves as non-racist are comfortable with lives where they have no contact with black people or where fear is their first response in any encounter with blackness. This 'fear' is the first sign of the internalization in the white psyche of white supremacist sentiments." (*Killing Rage* 267–68)

In white supremacist capitalist patriarchy, Joe Tory and the other black comics see those two white folks who sit down front and other white folks as crazy because we live in fear. Tory goes on: "I think y'all get tired of all the black people taking over all your shit. . . . I see white people sitting home be like, 'The goddamn Negroes are taking over football, basketball, every goddamn thing. We got to think of something they won't do. Yeah, why don't we climb an ice mountain? They don't want to do that.'" And behind the joke is an awareness of what little space blacks actually possess, of what little power blacks actually hold, and of what little opportunity blacks actually have to escape from the structures of white supremacy. So why are white folks afraid? Quite simply, white folks live in fear of the minorities they oppress, in fear that African-Americans will change the exploitive systems they want to protect. To be fair, to be honest, I must rewrite what I've just written: I live in fear of the minorities I oppress, in fear that African-Americans will change the exploitive system I want to protect.

And I am crazy, according to the DEF comics, because of what I might do out of that fear. Comic Ronnie Long comments: "Did you ever notice the media has a good way of making brothers look bad. Ya ever watch the news or something and they show a brother going to jail in slow motion? Make him look bad." I have watched those images, witnessed those who have committed crimes being put away without thinking about how they are represented. I have watched those handcuffed, dressed in orange coveralls, be led away and felt some comfort. I have watched and seen class and race.

Comic Chris Rock jokes: "The O.J. shit is over. . . . He's free. Free. . . . I ain't seen white people that mad since they cancelled *M.A.S.H.*" Listening to Chris Rock, I remember hearing the statistics that a large majority of whites felt O.J. was guilty and that a large majority of blacks felt he was innocent. I remember the stunned silence in Bennigan's Restaurant when I heard the verdict read. I remember seeing television footage of blacks applauding when they heard the verdict. I cannot remember any black actors ever appearing on *M.A.S.H.* "See what they did with Michael Jackson," Joe Tory warns. "See what happens when you let the wrong white person in your house? See what happens? I ain't prejudice but some of them buggers ain't on your side all the time." I was surprised to learn that Tory did not assume Jackson's guilt, that Tory did not believe Michael could molest a child, that Tory did not hesitate to say, "If I was him I wouldn't have come back. I'd be like: Fuck America." I am, like all whites, the wrong white person.

> hooks: "Until all Americans demand that mass media no longer serve as the biggest propaganda machine for white supremacy, the socialization of everyone to subliminally absorb white supremacist attitudes and values will continue." (*Killing Rage* 116)

And black folks who act like white folks are crazy. Spotting a black woman with curly blond hair, Joe Tory says, "Goldy motherfucking Locks, how you doin'? What the fuck is all that about? . . . You look like a ghetto Ginger from Gilligan's Island. Goddamn! I don't believe this shit. I thought white people do crazy things." I study her, wondering if she feels she should have been called out, if she sees herself as justly accused, if she wishes to change.

> hooks: "Aping whites, assimilating their values (i.e., white supremacist attitudes and assumptions) was clearly the way to achieve material success." (*Killing Rage*110)

I see her as attractive. The blond against black is striking. I know that her hair is not natural. I feel uneasy with her disguise, with her disregard for the genuine, and then I hear Tory mock a white perspective, "No, no, she's a nigger." I cringe but do not feel that Tory has captured my response to her. Mine is worse, for she can, as far as I am concerned, pass. I would let her come over, become one of us, take her in as one of our own.

> hooks: "It [assimilation] is a strategy deeply rooted in the ideology of white supremacy and its advocates urge black people to negate blackness, to imitate racist white people so as to better absorb their values, their way of life. (*Killing Rage* 186)

Black and White Gaze

In white supremacist capitalist patriarchy, they are looking, seeing themselves, seeing themselves onstage and in life. That's why they are laughing, laughing at what the comics make ring true for them. They are clapping, jumping up and down, falling out of their seats. They are loose as a person who doesn't care who is looking. Together, they are free to respond, free to look. And I am feeling guilty as I watch them watch, wondering if I intrude. Feeling safe in the privacy of my home, I secretly peep, peering at what was never meant for my eyes.

I see bodies unlike the ones I've known. These bodies are mysterious, strange, dark. These bodies are receptive, ready to respond, ready to give. These bodies are alive, on edge, alert. These bodies are barely under control, barely able to contain themselves. These bodies are boisterous, festive, celebratory. These bodies are sensuous, reveling and luxuriating in the moment. These bodies are young, still eager to believe but positioned to protect. These bodies are connected in community. These bodies hold potentials I do not understand. I sit on the couch, flipper in hand.

In white supremacist capitalist patriarchy, do I sit ready with my flipper because my body does not know how to join with theirs? Do I sit ready with my flipper because my body lives in fear, fear of the unknown, the uncontrollable, the ungoverned? Do I sit ready with my flipper because I know race matters, because in seeing them, I see exotic others, untamed primitives, because if this is true, I am ashamed? Help me put down my flipper, bell. Help me see what I should be seeing.

hooks: "While it has become 'cool' for white folks to hang out with black people and express pleasure in black culture, most white people do not feel that this pleasure should be linked to unlearning racism." (*Killing Rage* 157)

I am not trying to be cool. I want to unlearn racism, but I hear laughter, an electric laughter lighting the night. This laughter is volcanic, erupting from deep within and pushing aside the day's ash; it is molten. This laughter is contagious, spreading rapidly through the crowd. This laughter comes quick as a wink. This laughter is vociferous, obstreperous, uproarious. This laughter is unruly. This laughter knows no bounds, no restraints, no censors. This laughter is a tornado, tossing and twisting bodies until it settles into the pounding of applause. I do not participate.

In white supremacist capitalist patriarchy, do I not participate because I am not there—comics are always funnier when listening in a crowd? Do I not participate because I do not know how, do not know the rules, do not know what I need to know? Do I not participate because I do not approve—the sexism, the language, the jokes at others' expense? Do I not participate because to join in would be to surrender, to squander my position of privilege? Do I not participate because of fear of what I might become, of what I might lose? Help me bell, help me see.

hooks: "The truth is that many folks benefit greatly from dominating others and are not suffering a wound that is in any way similar to the condition of the exploited and oppressed." (*Killing Rage* 152)

I do not wish to benefit from dominating others. I will listen as you speak of exploitation and oppression. I will try to see them seeing themselves. To start again: They are looking, seeing themselves, seeing themselves onstage and in life. They see black and take comfort in color, in numbers, in sharing space.

hooks: "Those of us who remember living in the midst of racial apartheid know that the separate spaces, the times apart from whiteness, were for sanctuary, for reimagining and remembering ourselves." (*Killing Rage* 6)

This is their territory, where all others occupy the margins, all others are marginalized. They are center. They see themselves created, named, made before their eyes by themselves. They applaud their time to speak. They are claiming culture. They place their bodies in that space for their spirits and for their laughter that accepts who they are and challenges them. They listen without thoughts such as these because in this space they have the luxury of living for a moment in blackness, in community.

hooks: "That all attempts to repress our/black peoples' right to gaze had produced in us an overwhelming longing to look, a rebellious desire, an oppositional gaze. By courageously looking, we defiantly declared: 'Not only will I stare. I want my look to change reality.'" (*Black Looks* 116)

And I know that their stare, their oppositional gaze, is the most pleasing and the most powerful when I am rendered invisible. Yet, I want to say that there are things they are not seeing, that they are blind to how they work against their own interests. Can I point to this blindness with bell's help without her pointing at me?

hooks: "Bluntly put, as long as white scholars feel that they are doing black folks a favor when they critically engage black culture or that they necessarily know more than any black could ever know, then racism remains unchanged." (*Art on My Mind* 116)

This is not a favor, nor a statement of superior truth; it is a personal necessity, my search in white supremacist capitalist patriarchy for justice.

Language

Comic Ronnie Long compares:

White guys got *Playboy*, *Penthouse*, and *Hustler*. Know what brothers got? *Players* magazine—the lowest, dirtiest, nastiest magazine on the face of the earth. . . . You get *Playboy* and the girls are posed all nice and sexy. They got pumps on, fishnets, asses all out. And pussy hair is combed. It's like pussy's got a perm. You get *Players* and the girls are all mad because they're only getting ten dollars and their pimp is taking eight. They all mad. Pussy's got dandruff and bald spot.

In white supremacist capitalist patriarchy, such talk strikes me as vulgar. It is vulgar in that the language is crass, coarse, uncalled for, even in a comic frame. It is vulgar in that it accepts without question the practice of displaying women for the pleasure of men, of reducing women to their genitalia. It is vulgar in that it supports the notion that men, particularly pimps, might live off of the labor of women. It is vulgar in that it implies white women possess an aesthetic beauty beyond that of black women. It is vulgar in that everyone who is listening, including me, seems to find what Ronnie Long says, funny.

I laugh despite myself, perhaps enjoying the blatant disregard for correctness. I welcome the time to forget how I might offend, to set aside responsibility for my own talk and actions, to take off my white, middle-class, liberal boots. I laugh because I am in a position to do so. No one is looking. No one will hold me accountable. Except, I hear bell:

> hooks: "Progressive struggle to end white supremacy recognizes the political importance of accountability. . . ."(*Killing Rage* 61)

I laugh at all the right places for all the wrong reasons. But perhaps I am being dismissive too quickly. Perhaps there are words in Ronnie Long's routine that redeem, words that resist. Perhaps, I should simply celebrate his courage to speak, his claiming of public space.

> hooks: "I was afraid of saying the wrong thing. Fear of saying or doing that which will be considered 'wrong' often inhibits people who are members of exploited and/or oppressed groups. This inhibiting factor acts to suppress and stifle creativity both in terms of critical thinking and artistic expression." (*Talking Back* 161)

Ronnie Long does not seem inhibited, and I cannot find a moment I want to applaud. I hear bell hooks speaking, but I do not believe that she speaks for Ronnie Long. Nor, at this moment, does she speak for me. Her fear is different. It is not my fear of being caught acting politically incorrect. My fear has the protection of power. At worst, I might lose some regard from those I oppress. I am still the one who names.

> hooks: "The oppressed struggle in language to recover ourselves—to rewrite, to reconcile, to renew. Our words are not without meaning. They are an action—a resistance. Language is . . . a place of struggle." (*Talking Back* 28)

Still, I cannot see the value in Ronnie Long's words. Nor can I justify my laughter. He provides no words of comfort, no space I want to occupy, no resistant action. I think you would agree, bell, that black talk, just because it is black talk, is not enough for social change. But as I listen more closely to other moments of the *DEF Jam*, I have reason to believe that language may be a site of struggle.

When their routines are filled with African-American patois, I hear more than nonstandard speech. Even though I am at times jolted by "incorrect" grammar, shut out by language I do not know, or surprised by discourse taboos, I recognize the power of such linguistic play. These strategies help African-Americans in the search for their own identity, their own community. With such strategies, language becomes a tool of resistance rather than a weapon deployed against them. Such strategies allow African-Americans to control language, to establish their own grammar, to name their own desires.

When their routines use language to help us see, I hear more than the cry of victims. I hear voices calling us to action, calling us forward in the ongoing struggle. When the audience loudly applauds Muggah's comic critique of men's sexist behavior as she ends her routine saying, "That'll teach you brothers that we are not bitches and whores. We're your lovers, wives and mothers of your children," the healing potential of verbal art becomes evident. At such times, I believe that change is possible.

> hooks: "By transforming the oppressor's language, making a culture of resistance, black people created an intimate speech that could say far more than was permissible within the boundaries of standard English. The power of this speech is not simply that it enables resistance to white supremacy, but that it also forges a space for alternative cultural production and alternative epistemologies—different ways of thinking and knowing that were crucial to creating a counter-hegemonic worldview." (*Teaching to Transgress* 171)

When their routines end with "You all be careful," "God bless you and good night," and "Peace," I hear more than clichés. Such closures are calls to community, marking a shared space where we might begin to speak not as a unitary voice but as members of the human collective who long for equality and mutual respect. Such closures point to the desire that humans fair well in the company of each other, that they find solace in the good will of each other. As I listen to the comics' routines their endings promise beginnings, beginnings not anchored in white supremacist capitalist patriarchy but in the desire for social justice.

> hooks: "Naming is a serious process. It has been of crucial concern for many individuals within oppositional groups who struggle for self-recovery, for self-determination." (*Talking Back* 166)

Still, as I watch the *DEF Comedy Jam* I am troubled. I want to alter how men and women name each other. I want to reflect upon my own thoughts, my own inappropriate laughter.

Sex and Sexism

In white supremacist capitalist patriarchy, I am pulled in by the talk of sex—raw, explicit details that elicit roars of laughter. They joke about sexual intercourse, heterosexual and homosexual sex, cunnilingus, fellatio, bondage, and prostitution. They joke about sexual subjects I've been told one doesn't discuss, subjects I've been told are not proper in mixed company, are not proper even in the bedroom. They joke about techniques, about who is willing to do what to whom. They joke about black prowess and white inadequacy. They joke about how the body looks, sounds, feels, tastes, smells. They joke about bodies for free and bodies for sale. For the most part, these are men's jokes, jokes at the expense of women.

I know the feminist critique: women reduced to objects, to commodities, serving the pleasure of men; women diminished by the male gaze, subject to men's degrading and silencing leers; women valued only for their sexual favors and then discarded like spoiled meat. As I watch, this critique is present, available, easy. It is important, essential; but I place it on hold, suspended above my viewing. Only then can I laugh. Yet, I know that this laughter has a price, one that we all must pay as we perpetuate patriarchy. And I know that sexism is only one of several structures of domination.

> hooks: "Since all forms of oppression are linked in our society because they are supported by similar institutional and social structures, one system cannot be eradicated while others remain intact." (*Feminist Theory* 35)

So I look again at how I process the comic's talk of black sexuality, not to see the feminist issues, not to acknowledge my own sexism (this I think I know) but to place race and sex in front of me.

In white supremacist capitalist patriarchy, I know better than my own thoughts and feelings that emerge when I watch. For I slip into all the stereotypes, all the absurd mystifications, all the traps of racist thinking. For when I hear the comics talk of blacks and sex, I compare those images to those I hold for white sexuality. I wonder in my racist mind if blacks are more active, more open, more promiscuous than whites. Their sexuality seems apparent, always in negotiation. They seem eager for their next encounter. They seem to know how to live in the pleasures of their body. They seem to know what they want. Such prurient thoughts play on the imagination, casting black sexuality as the forbidden fruit. Even worse, such ideas turn blacks into amoral beasts who pursue their carnal desires without conscious.

> hooks: "For black bodies, the fear has not been losing touch with our carnality and physicality but how to be in touch with our bodies in a way that is liberatory, that does not confine us to racist/sexist paradigms of subjugated embodiment." (*Art on My Mind* 204)

In white supremacist capitalist patriarchy, the DEF comics are not offering discourse that liberates. When Montana Taylor jokes, "All you cows got men? Where dey at? I tell you where dey at. They're at home like, 'Oh she went to the *DEF Jam*, baby. We got plenty of time,'" she is perpetuating the system. When Tony Brown calls out, "You know there are some phony titties in the room," he is perpetuating the system. When Daryl Heat claims, "Everybody's pimping these days. I saw a midget pimp," he is perpetuating the system. When Chris Rock says, "I would never hit a woman, but I'd shake the shit out of a woman, like, 'What the fuck is wrong with you,'" he is perpetuating the system. I perpetuate the system when I watch and laugh.

> hooks: "Revolutionary feminism embraces men who are able to change, who are capable of responding mutually in a subject-to-subject encounter where desire and fulfillment are in no way linked to coercive subjugation. This feminist vision of the sexual imaginary is the space few men seem able to enter." (*Outlaw Culture* 81)

Classism, Sexism, and Racism

In white supremacist capitalist patriarchy, sex is linked with class. It is what "nice girls" don't do. It is what makes "girls" cheap, low rent. It is, as I watch the *DEF Jam* late on a Saturday night on one of my three televisions, safe in my middle-class home in my middle-class neighborhood near my middle-class university with my middle-class daughter locked inside, what I am not doing with my middle-class wife. And since black girls aren't nice girls, black girls do it. Such classist, sexist, and racist thoughts are part of many whites' cultural heritage, a heritage deeply ingrained in their white daughters and sons. Such thoughts were told to daughters to protect them from men and told to sons to enhance their sexual exploits with women. Such thoughts implicate morality with class, sex, and race, placing, of course, white middle-class men alone on the moral high ground. And when someone might dare to aim a moral question at men, well, boys will be boys.

In white supremacist capitalist patriarchy, I can maneuver easily around these obvious roadblocks to equality. It is not difficult to recognize the troubling logics set up between men and women, blacks and whites, and the low and middle classes. Yet, as I listen to the comics their jokes take me back to those roadblocks. Rudy Rush teases about the roaches in his woman friend's apartment that have been "lifting weights." Sedjack wisecracks that you know you are in a black neighborhood when you see "a church, a liquor store, a Chinese restaurant, and a cash checkin' place." Donald Curry laughs about getting behind a "raggedy ass Cadillac" in a drive-through. Ronnie Long says that Brooklyn is such a wild scene that he saw this "black guy robbin' his own self." Dominique drops to the bottom line: "Ain't nothin' worse than a broke ass man." What truths do I see in these jokes? What stereotypes do they reinforce? Is an individual's worth measured in money? Answering such questions, I move with caution, afraid of what sense I might make of the facts, afraid of what the facts might suggest I should do.

> hooks: "To confront class in black life in the United States means that we must deconstruct the notion of an essential binding blackness and be able to critically examine ways the desire to be accepted into privileged-class groups within mainstream society undermines and at times destroys commitment to a politics of cultural transformation that consistently critiques domination. Such a critique would necessarily include the challenge to end class elitism and call for replacing the ethic of individualism with a vision of communalism." (*Killing Rage* 175–76)

I don't know, bell, if I can go where the facts lead you. I don't know if communalism is the answer. I don't know if by embracing communalism we can end oppression. I don't know if I am willing to give up what I have, what I've worked for. I don't know if I am willing to take on transformational politics that hurt me. I can act as if I'm not sexist, racist, or classist by watching what I say and by arguing for equal opportunities and justice. But how much of my wealth am I willing to share? And does sharing my wealth mean increased contact? Does it mean I would be one of them?

White Supremacist Capitalist Patriarchy

I am a white supremacist in capitalist patriarchy. I fear becoming one of them, becoming a "broke ass man," becoming one of the "have-nots." I've come to see that I want my encounters safe—on the pages of books, on television programs and films, or with those who are like me, who hold the same membership cards. In my anthropological gaze, I want all the comforts of home. I want to keep my distance so that I might speak my liberal views and receive all the benefits of being so tolerant. I want the benefits of writing this essay, of saying I am a white supremacist in capitalist patriarchy.

The DEF comics joke about themselves and make me think about my relationship to them, about how I witness them and about what I value. I know that often I do not agree with what they think it means to be cool, to be DEF. It is not DEF to present jokes that continue the commodification and subjugation of women, that reinforce the coercive hierarchies

145

that subordinate all peoples of color, and that fail to interrogate and disrupt the status quo. It is not DEF for me to laugh when I hear their jokes. I am not cool when I fail to dismantle systems of oppression, fail to intervene and transform.

In white supremacist capitalist patriarchy, I appropriate bell hooks's phrase: white supremacist capitalist patriarchy. I try to write without white male guilt, without my writing becoming another hegemonic gesture. I cannot. I need to talk, perhaps only over in the corner with others of my kind so that we will not take up too much room. I need to listen to those I oppress so that I might change my ways. I need to watch myself watching so that I might escape my own colonizing eyes and uncover what I need to see. Your phrase, bell, has helped me to see, to recognize what must be done. But I am frozen, unable to move. I cannot shed my fear nor trust all of your solutions. I think that is because I am a white supremacist in capitalist patriarchy.

> hooks: "Some days it is just hard to accept that racism can still be such a powerful dominating force in all our lives." (*Killing Rage* 263)

Bibliography of Works by bell hooks

Art on My Mind: Visual Politics. New York: The New Press, 1995.
Black Looks: Race and Representation. Boston: South End Press, 1992.
Feminist Theory: From Margin to Center. Boston: South End Press, 1984.
Killing Rage: Ending Racism. New York: Henry Holt, 1995.
Outlaw Culture: Resisting Representations. New York: Routledge, 1994.
Talking Back: Thinking Feminist, Thinking Black. Boston: South End Press, 1989.
Teaching to Transgress: Education as the Practice of Freedom. New York: Routledge, 1994.
Yearning: Race, Gender, and Cultural Politics. Boston: South End Press, 1990.

14
Moving Bodies in Space and Time

Relax. This isn't difficult. Together, we can figure it out. Put your pencil down. No need to take notes. When you are ready, we can begin.

This is an examination of acting and directing, of moving bodies in space and time, and of bodies that were emotionally moving, directing their audiences over space and time to live in the power of their claims. In this essay, I explore the difficulty and ethics of accomplishing the latter while doing the former. In short, I am interested in the construction and interpretation of semiotic codes.

Nothing much there. Just a typical guiding concept. Keep going. It gets more interesting as you continue. Look at scene 1.

Scene 1: Getting Oriented

He was a new student to the doctoral program, an older, large man who hadn't said anything in the performance art class during the first two weeks. No one seemed to know anything about this strange man who appeared on the first day of summer session, looking intense, serious, and introspective, and who furiously took notes on everything, from the most trivial passing comment to passages from the first book being read for the term, C. Carr's *On Edge: Performance at the End of the Twentieth Century*. When it was his turn to perform, no one knew what to expect.

The stage was set with a small table and lamp beside a large cushioned chair, upstage right. On the table was a bottle of wine, a wine glass, and an ashtray. Down center was a wooden desk, desk chair, and lamp. The light was dim as he entered, lit a cigarette, and sat in the upstage chair. He turned on the lamp and poured himself some wine. He drank and smoked in silence; he drank and smoked for several minutes. When he finished his cigarette, he put it out and turned off the lamp. Then, he slowly got up, moved down center to the desk, and turned on the desk lamp. He reached into the desk drawer, pulled out a gun, and placed it to his temple. He seemed calm and determined. He cocked the gun. He held the cocked pistol to his temple for perhaps twenty seconds before he slowly pulled it away. He stared at it and placed it back in the desk drawer. He turned off the desk lamp and returned to the upstage chair. He repeated the process five times; the performance lasted over thirty minutes.

As the performance continued the audience sat still. They were unsure if what they were witnessing was a performance. Perhaps, they wondered, he is going to shoot himself. No one in the audience knew him well; no one knew if the gun was real or loaded; no one knew if he was capable of pulling the trigger. And, no one moved. No one went onstage to say, "Enough. I'm not sure what is going on here, but I'll not be a part of a suicide." It would have been easy to do. The stage was quite accessible; the gun could have been taken away; the performance was only a classroom project. And I, the instructor for the course, sat with them, watching.

The point to note here, of course, is the power of theatrical conventions. That is all actors and directors have. They can work with them or against them, but they are never absent. That is all audiences have. Did you trust that I would not tell about this performance if he had actually shot himself? Did you believe his suicide would be too sensational for the beginning of our time together? Or, is the point to note here a question of ethical responsibility? Are you horrified that no one, particularly the instructor, tried to stop the performance? What obligations does one have as a witness? What obligations do you take on? Please proceed.

The convention program was in memory of those who had died of AIDS. The performers, I believe all gay, presented poems, stories, and scenes from plays that tell about AIDS. The performances were filled with anger. They were disturbing, moving. The performance that remains etched in my mind, however, was that of Timothy Gura, who did a scene from Anderson Ferrell's novel entitled *Home for the Day*. The part he selected to perform is Fred's story of Pete, his lover for seventeen years who died in his arms. We learn that Pete was a professional tap dancer, an outstanding talent whose career guided their lives. After each performance, Pete would ask Fred, "Do you still love me?" When Pete became ill, they decided that they wanted him to die at home. The final paragraphs of the scene read:

> Before he died, he became lucid again. Basically he bled to death. Late in the afternoon, I saw a dark cloud, brown and red and black, spread out from under him on the sheet. At first, I tried to clean it up, but it kept coming so I thought I'd do it later. I just got in bed with him, sat up against the headboard and pulled him up into my arms. Before long the sheets were soaked, and I could hear what was coming out of Pete dripping onto the floor.

Just before he went, he tried to crane his neck back to look at me, so I shifted around, still holding him, to where he could see me. His eyes twinkled mischievously, as though he had played a trick on me and was waiting for me to find out, and I thought I saw something like a smile on his cracked lips. Then they parted, and his tongue searched for the place where words were kept, and when it found a place near there, he spoke.

"Still love me now?" he asked. He sounded like a little boy who has done something bad but knows he is adorable anyway.

"Oh, yeah. Oh yeah," I said.

These words come into you almost without warning, settling inside, refusing to leave. They stake a claim. And when they come from a performer as skilled as Timothy Gura, they take shape in his body. Tim is Fred, holding Pete in front of us, displaying the love one man can have for another. And when Tim reaches the final line and chooses not to bury his head in his hands but to throw his head back as he cries out, "Oh yeah. Oh yeah," so that we might see the pain written across his face, we know that in these lives, Pete's, Fred's, and Tim's, we are implicated.

Allow yourself time to imagine that scene. Allow yourself time to respond. Allow yourself time to act. If you cannot, perhaps you are not the person we need. Feel free to stop.

Scene 2: Choosing the Right Side

I was pleased to be invited as a directorial eye to a rehearsal of her one-woman show. She was literalizing the metaphor of placing herself in someone else's shoes to guide her from character to character. To set this framework, she started the show musing over a pile of shoes. As I watched, I felt her characterizations were solid, needing only a gentle nudge here or a slight push there. She was having difficulty, however, scripting the opening. She needed help with the pile of shoes. We started playing in the pile, improvising, searching for lines that might work. I picked up an American Indian moccasin, put my hand inside, and had the shoe prance around while making the stereotypic war call. With the other hand, I picked up a cowboy boot by the toe and smashed it into the moccasin. We laughed and the bit became a part in the show. Several members of the audience were offended.

There is no escape from politics. Make sure you select the correct side. Make sure you know where to stand. Make sure you are not at risk. Always remember, something or somebody is at stake. Choose.

Relationships was a show about couples, how they live their lives, how they work out their problems. Act I featured five couples struggling to make sense of their relationships. Act II provided the audience a chance to engage in improvisational scenes with the cast about relational problems they have experienced. When he came onstage, the cast sensed he was distraught. He wanted to play the role of the injured party in a scene about infidelity. The cast set up the scenario. He began by simply saying to the actor playing the role of the cheating partner, "How could you? How could you?" When she answered, "It just happened," he started a rambling, incoherent speech about his love for her. She tried to break in, but he was shouting, irrational, and then he broke down crying. The cast acted quickly. One actor worked the crowd, saying how relationship issues are often intense and asking how alternative relational strategies might have proven more effective. Another comforted him and guided him out into the theatre lobby. He was sent on his way. The cast knew just what was needed to save the moment, to let the show go on.

Choose again. Save the show or save the man? It seems an easy ethical choice, but remember, once you've committed to playing with such themes in that format, you may encounter what you cannot handle. Do you know how to save the man? Perhaps the man was saved by his own venting, by the supportive hug he received as he was led from the theatre. Perhaps he was better off after the event. Perhaps he was not.

Scene 3: Deciding Where to Stand

"I'm uncomfortable," she said, "taking the Lord's name in vain."

It was hard for me to believe that anyone in theatre would have difficulty with this language. My response was quick and predictable: "I can understand your feelings, but it isn't you that is taking the Lord's name in vain. It's the character. Those words help demonstrate who this character is."

"I know it is the character who is speaking," she answered, "but I just don't want to say those words."

Let's try something. Imagine yourself cast in a show. You have heard over the years of the transformative power of performance and of how performance offers alternative life scripts. You believe, as you were taught to believe, that you cannot perform a character without in some way being changed by that experience. You are asked to do something that you do not wish to do, that is against your own ethical principles. Complete the following sentence: I am willing to get onstage, but I am unwilling to. . . . Make your list. Under what circumstances might you go against your own wishes?

It was clear from the beginning: Being in the show required being nude.

If you were uncomfortable with nudity, you shouldn't audition. When he said to her that he would like to see her audition, she was flattered. His invitation was coded to suggest that if she auditioned, she would get a part. She admired him and wanted a chance to be in one of his productions. This was an opportunity she felt she could not miss. Yet, she could not see herself nude onstage, particularly in a play where the nudity and intimacy between characters seemed gratuitous and particularly in a theatre where the audience was so close.

She approached him: "Does everyone in the cast have to be nude?"

"Yes," he answered. "Do you have a problem with that?"

The way he asked the question made her feel small, unprofessional. "No," she replied, knowing now that she had to audition.

Read the rewritten description below. Notice the difference when the actor decides to audition because of economic necessity.

It was clear from the beginning: Being in the show required being nude. If you were uncomfortable with nudity, you shouldn't audition. When he said to her that he would like to see her audition, she was relieved. His invitation was coded to suggest that if she auditioned, she would get a part. She needed the work. This was a chance for her to get back on her feet. Yet, she could not see herself nude onstage, particularly in a play where the nudity and intimacy between characters seemed gratuitous and particularly in a theatre where the audience was so close.

She approached him: "Does everyone in the cast have to be nude?"

"Yes," he answered. "Do you have a problem with that?"

The way he asked the question made her feel as if she were replaceable. "No," she replied, knowing that she had to audition.

Remember: Being ethical is easy when you have power.

Perhaps you need some space to respond, to contribute to the final product. Perhaps I've been too much in control, too directive, too dogmatic. I don't want to stifle your creativity. Please feel free to offer any thoughts you might have. I believe that this can only work when everyone is working toward the same end. So please, just jump in when you feel the need.

Scene 4:

(Include your favorite example here. I really do want your input. Then cross straight down, page left, to scene 5.)

Scene 5: Power

Romance was a show about desire. It consisted of three scenes adapted from romance novels, staged respectively as realism, melodrama, and farce, stories written and performed by the cast, about their own personal relationships with others, and critical commentary, most often feminist, about the romance genre. It was important to me that the show was inclusive, that it not simply feature heterosexual desire. In addition to including narratives about homosexual and bisexual romantic lives, I cast three women for the farcical romance novel scene, a scene originally written as the typical climactic moment, when a man and a woman decide they must have one another. One woman was cast as a voyeuristic narrator who is intent on watching and telling about the intimate lives of two lovers. The second woman played the role of a beautiful and seductive heroine who cannot keep her hands off of her lover. The third woman worked from behind a life-size cardboard cutout of Fabio, speaking and moving as the stereotypical macho-man. Midway through the scene, she is overcome by her lover's passion and discards the Fabio cutout. The scene ends with the three women on the floor in a simulated orgiastic and orgasmic climax. Behind the farce was a serious intent. I wanted to demonstrate, coded in part by the discarding of the Fabio cutout, that only through abandoning the rigid structures of compulsory heterosexuality can lesbian desire obtain its fullest potential.

Problems arose immediately. First, none of the women I cast happened to be lesbian, and one woman felt uncomfortable playing a lesbian role. Second, two of the women had limited experience with issues of sexual politics and questioned if such a scene was actually needed or appropriate for the show. Third, I, a man, became the dramaturg on lesbian desire. In the end, I used my position as director to insist that the scene not only remain in the production but be staged how I envisioned it.

In final analysis, I wonder if I ever convinced the cast that the scene served an important function in the show. I wonder if the women, by enacting lesbian desire onstage, enhanced lesbian interests. I wonder if a number of the audience members, many of whom were undergraduate students required to attend the production, simply read the scene as a farce, as a good laugh at those dikes. I wonder if I was only staging my own desire.

When you have power, use it. When you have power, don't abuse it. These are never easy mandates.

Stop if you are unhappy. You don't have to deal with another word. Perhaps you're bored. Perhaps you have other things you need to do. Perhaps you are offended. Whatever the case, you are free to choose. I only ask that you remember that I am trying. I am giving you the best I have. Perhaps you feel that is not enough. I know I've made mistakes. I'm sure I will make more. For that, I ask your forgiveness and generosity of spirit.

Perhaps you are not in a forgiving mood. Perhaps you are not kind. Perhaps you do not wish to go on to scene 6?

Scene 6: Finding What's Needed

The power of David Henry Hwang's *M. Butterfly* rests in being convinced that you could have been seduced by Song Liling, that you could find yourself, as René Gallimard did, in love and making love with a man disguised as a woman, without knowing he was a man, that you could become the object of ridicule by your simple desire to love another. It is in being persuaded when Song explains to the Judge, "You expect Oriental countries to submit to your guns, and you expect Oriental women to be submissive to your men," and when she says, "Only a man knows how a woman is supposed to act." It is in being moved by it all. After Gallimard's magical transformation into M. Butterfly in the final scene, after he plunges a knife into his body, and after Song calls out in a chilling inquiry, "Butterfly? Butterfly?" its power is in allowing yourself to cry.

Keep going. I know it may be difficult to get to the heart of this the first time, but we need to see where we are, to discover what are the problem spots, to identify where else we have to go.

My intent was pure. I swear. I just wanted to help the show. So, when I saw his character Sally Tassie Tallahassee portraying all the roles in her one person show of *Hedda Gabler*, I wanted to make her more convincing, more female. I was, I've come to see in retrospect, trying to turn his camp character into an object I could desire. I detailed from years of observation and demonstrated with my large heterosexual body how she might be more like a woman. I wanted, like Gallimard, to become "a man who loved a woman created by a man." I forgot how a man might create a man dressed as a woman for a man. Blinded by my heterosexual presumption, this was an idea I did not know how to direct.

Can the rough edges be taken off? Can we move closer to what we want? Can we get it right? Remember why we are here. Let's move on.

It is a simple example, part of a larger work entitled *Straight M[eye]nd*, written and performed by Craig Gingrich-Philbrook. The opening reads:

> I was sitting in Denny's restaurant the other night and overheard a woman say, "Bob's queer you know. He told everyone. He even had the nerve to introduce his lover at the Christmas party. Can you believe it. Can you believe that guy. God, he just flaunts it."

Of course, this attitude made me rather angry, so I turned around to look at this person, to see what a bigot looks like. And in this case, let me tell you: a bigot looks just like a lot of you:

Nice.

She looked nice.

And the thing was, without thinking, she had put her arm around her boyfriend's shoulders—yeah, right there in Denny's, she was sitting there, running her fingers through her boyfriend's hair, <u>right there in Denny's.</u> Can you believe it. Can you believe that woman? She was <u>flaunting it. Flaunting it, her nice bigot self. But that's straight m[eye]nd for you. The faggots are always flaunting it, but the bigots, well, the bigots are just living their lives.</u>

I cannot touch my wife in public without thinking of this example, without remembering my privilege as a heterosexual man, without guilt. I am in his debt. I am a different man.

Perhaps we have spent enough time here. I would, however, like you to think about this in case we decide to go through it again. For now, we need to turn our attention to other matters. Scene 7 is something for us to work on.

Scene 7: Making Judgments

Ronald Frederickson's performance of Robert Browning's "My Last Duchess" was definitive. It was simply perfect: a casual and commanding character who enjoys his station, a man of manners and words speaking with the ease of one who need never question, a person blind to his own inadequacies. It was a performance that rendered all previous ones suspect and that would be the measure against which all future ones would be judged. The audience knew, without question and without a single voice of resistance, what they had witnessed: a performance so compelling, so accurate, so skilled that they would always remember the Duke of Ferrara not as Browning's creation but as Frederickson's.

At times, your permission to go with the moment is taken away by its sheer power. At other times, you must grant permission, even force yourself into the experience. At other times, you must withhold your permission, resist as if your life depended upon it. It does.

Lesa Lockford's performance piece was entitled "Spin the Ideological Bottle." The audience members, arranged in a circle, were central to this carefully planned game show. The piece was set to the music of Eartha Kitt's version of "Love for Sale" and Tom Waits's "Step Right Up." The host, a Vanna White-like character dressed in short black skirt and top, would spin a full Coke bottle. The audience member who was isolated by the pointing bottle was given a question on feminist history. The questions were not difficult or obscure; they were taken from an undergraduate final examination in a women's study class. But even for an audience with considerable experience in feminist scholarship, no one answered any question correctly. When an audience member failed to answer a question, the host took off a piece of her clothing and gave it to that audience member. The bottle spun again and the process continued until the host was stripped, except for gauze across her breasts and around her pelvic area. Written on the gauze in front was "We Get What We Pay For" and on the back, "Damaged Goods." Then, without saying a word, the host made a complete circle, arms outstretched, directly in front of each audience member. After locating and displaying the Coke bottle, she snapped off the cap with a bottle opener pulled from and attached to a string in her pelvic area. She fell to her knees, lifted the Coke bottle well above her, and turned her head up to take in the pouring Coke. The Coke came quickly and splashed over her face and body.

The piece was disturbing. Audience members felt trapped, unable to free themselves from the game show frame. The images, particularly the last one, seemed violent, obscene. The message—that our failure to recognize women's history perpetuates women's oppression and objectification—was familiar but became visceral and concrete as audience members were handed pieces of clothing and witnessed the consequences of their ignorance. In short, by playing the game, the audience becomes implicated in the oppression of women. The game becomes increasingly uncomfortable as the audience sees in bolder and bolder terms the results of their stupidity.

The bottle is pointing. Select one: You believe you would have (a) become swept away by this event, (b) made yourself deal with what was presented, or (c) resisted. Which option do you pick? The correct choice is "b." Did you, like everyone else who witnessed this piece, want to select "c"?

The piece, Tracy Stephenson's "Me & You (Part Two): Redeconstruction," was about breast reduction. The words were nothing more than a medical explanation adapted from a pamphlet entitled *Breast Reduction: Reduction Mamaplasty.* Adapted, the opening read:

Taken from the Greek word plastikos, which means to mold or give form, plastic surgery is a specialty that makes it possible to do just that: mold or reform the human body. Procedures that heal and restore patients with deformities from injury, disease or birth defect are called *reconstructive*. Those that change or enhance the appearance by recontouring facial or body features are called *aesthetic*.

The performance, however, was much more than its words. First, Stephenson placed these words in a theatrical frame and played them to a small, intimate audience who knew prior to the event that she had had a breast reduction. Second, as she began speaking, she removed her top, full front, and, after some time, proceeded to put on a medical gown that positioned one breast ready for surgery. As she continued, she wrote on her breast, indicating where incisions would be made and highlighting where scars would remain.

Perhaps it was the fact that the audience saw all her actions played out on her own body, a body that they knew had undergone this procedure, that made the performance work. Perhaps it was that the audience knew the performer and could not forget the person behind the medical jargon that made it work. Perhaps it was seeing a woman expose her breasts for public gaze and, then, witnessing the transformation of breasts from fetishized objects into medical ones that made it work. Perhaps it was because she was my student, a student with whom I'd adopted a paternal relationship, that I wanted to stop the performance and to deny any interest.

Do you have any questions? Do I share too much?
It is too late to consider quitting. We only have a short time before it's all over. You have already made a considerable investment. So have I. I would hate to see that wasted. I hope you decide to stick it out. Perhaps we can incorporate more of your ideas.

Scene 8:

(Incorporate what you think is needed here.)

Scene 9: Knowing What to Expect

I tried everything I knew how to do. We started, of course, in a typical fashion: We read the script together, discussed various interpretations, and settled on a vision for his character. We worked from his initial efforts. At first, the fact that his efforts were so inadequate was not particularly bothersome. We had plenty of time. I offered suggestions, words that might set him in the right direction, metaphors that might trigger meaningful connections. I placed him in improvisations designed to enrich his understanding of the character. I was supportive, encouraging him at every turn. I tried backing off, giving him some space to find what was needed. I asked him what he thought might help and pursued his suggestions. I brought in a colleague to help. I functioned as an acting coach, as a psychologist, as a tolerant parent. As the opening night approached, I knew we wouldn't achieve what we wanted. I narrowed the vision in the hopes that he might achieve a less ambitious goal. I cut some lines. I isolated one key aspect of the character that I wanted him to display. We felt frustrated, discouraged. We were striving for what might pass as adequate.

Opening night, he was still awful. He asked me how he did. "Fine," I said. He grinned and handed me a card. Enclosed was a three-page, single-spaced letter saying how personally meaningful the show had been for him. I believed him. No one liked the show.

Meeting expectations is a question of where you sit. Perhaps you need to change locations?

I wanted the structure of my show on concrete poetry to mirror its form. I was particularly interested in playing with the repetition of visual and auditory typographical arrangements common with concrete poetry. My solution was to have Act II duplicate Act I, except that Act II would be run backwards. I explained the idea to the cast, making sure that the theoretical arguments were sound and the production concept was clear. They were skeptical but agreeable. Rehearsals went well: The production emerged polished, distinct, funny. Act I concluded with enthusiastic applause. But during Act II, they left, at first just a few when they recognized what was happening, then more, and finally, by the end, only a few audience members remained. The cast was devastated. No one expected them to leave.

Do you like where you are sitting? Do you like doing what you are doing? Knowing what you know now, would you like to get up, change positions, take on a different role? Leave?

I wanted to generate a performance piece about the creation of stories. I was interested in how stories are formed, bounce against one another, and stay with us. I was particularly intrigued by what might happen if a highly self-reflexive story structure were put into operation, and having done so, what might become evident about how stories function. I arranged for a convention slot and sent out two invitations to fifteen different colleagues. The first read:

This is a performance piece entitled
"Story"
Please remember:
your thoughts on being cast in this story,
whatever you might say to others about this, and
what they might say to you

The second read:

You are cordially invited to perform
"Story"
The 62nd Annual Convention of the
Central States Communication Association

Oklahoma City, Oklahoma
Friday, April 8, 1994
10:15–11:45
19th Century Room, Century Center

The performance piece will be divided into two parts:
"On Being Cast"
"Tales We Tell"

Please prepare a short monologue on these themes.
There are no rules.
BYOP: Bring Your Own Props

Ten colleagues developed tales to tell. They were highly creative, imaginative performances that had the audience in stitches. They had very little in common except that I was often referenced, a detail that I did not expect. I was embarrassed. I had arranged a program not centering, as I had intended, on how stories might come into being and how they might structure limited information into compelling events but often focusing on me. Every story needs an antagonist.

Have we spent too much time together? Did you get what you expected? Have you had enough of me? What is your story? It is never too late to add in more. Are you ready for it to end? If so, cross down to scene 10.

Scene 10: Openings and Closings

Anna Deavere Smith's *Fires in the Mirror* is a magnificent achievement. The critics, as quoted on the 1993 Anchor Books edition of the play, were unanimous. Frank Rick of the *New York Times* wrote, "Quite simply the most compelling and sophisticated view of urban racial and class conflict that one could hope to encounter." The *Wall Street Journal* announced, "An extraordinary play . . . riveting . . . an unsparing rendering of the myriad emotions of the [Crown Heights] incident." *New York Newsday* proclaimed, "Spellbinding. Deeply perceptive. Provocative. Throbs with understandable emotions on all sides." Others spoke in similar superlatives, and they were right. So, should I mention that as I watch and read about *Fires in the Mirror*, I think not about Crown Heights but about Anna Deavere Smith? Should I say that Anna Deavere Smith's *Fires in the Mirror* is about Anna Deavere Smith?

What makes for a good opening or a good closing? Do openings and closings have to have a dramatic kick that pulls you in and keeps you thinking? Where is your attention?

Out of Me We Speak was a show interested in displaying the actor's craft. Five actors selected two monologues to perform. Integrated with their performances of the monologues were commentaries about their processes as actors. The show was arranged to mirror a typical actor's process, moving from the first encounter with a script to the unwinding or separating from a character. The final piece in the production, an anonymous diary entry from an acute, highly distressed schizophrenic, was performed by Anita Rich. In the scene, the character, who is given the business of working with finger paints, becomes increasingly agitated and forgets that she has paint on her hands. As she speaks, she moves her hands to her face, and by the end of her utterance, she is covered with paint. Anita Rich gives herself over to this character; she becomes lost in the character's intense, frantic world. When the character stops speaking, Rich must unwind, return to herself. She moves center stage and uncovers a washing basin. The piece ends under a single light, with Rich's nonverbal commentary: the ritual cleansing, the washing away of the physical evidence, the letting go.

But, of course, it cannot be washed away or let go, or, at least, not completely. It lives on in memory, in image, in what is made of it. It takes a place in Rich's body as it does in the bodies of those who came to witness. It is a lesson to be learned. It is a burden to carry, a responsibility, and a prayer.

If this is going to come together, you will have to put in more effort. I've done everything I can. The lines are there for you. You just have to let them in. Remember the things we've talked about. Use your head. Don't be afraid to respond. It really is up to you if this is going to work. It is your choice.

15

An Interview

You have been working in performance for over thirty years now. I'm interested in any observations you might want to make about how you have come to understand the performance experience.

Well, I don't know if I can offer any simple summary. I have come to believe though that a key dimension is found in the relationship that a performer takes to words. First, I'd say that a performer cannot allow the words to remain on the page, as marks still awaiting evocation. Here, there is no relationship, no contact. But once contact is made, words seems to locate themselves differently in the performer. At times, it seems the words are in the performer's hands, cupped, and held out for both the performer's and the audience's admiration. The performer shares the words in a public act of appreciation. At times, it seems the words are in the performer's heart, deeply felt, filled with personal significance. The performer displays the import of the words to himself/herself as they are kept inside. They are taken in as one might swallow an antidepressant. At times, they are in the performer's head, either as a failure of memorization or as a celebration of craft. As a failure of memorization, the words seem to bounce around inside, struggle to take form, and fall from view. They are mistreated. As a celebration of craft, the words become an opportunity for technical display, for tricks of the trade, for virtuosity. The head watches the words dance but feels nothing. At times, the words are placed between the feet, ready to be kicked around, trampled. Here, the performer wants the audience to see why certain words won't do. At times, the words are on the tip of the finger, pointing. Here, the performer wants the audience to see why they won't do. I could go on, but I think the point should be clear: A performer establishes a bodily relationship to the words he/she utters, and that relationship may or may not be a productive one for the purposes of a given performance.

Do you see an analogue to everyday performance behavior?

Yes, it does seem to me that people tend to establish a primary relationship to words in their everyday lives. Of course, their relationship to words will shift at different times, but people adopt a basic bodily orientation to words, one that often helps characterize who they are. Sometimes people yield to words; sometimes they resist their power. Poet Karen Blomain writes, "Something pulls us into words." Whatever that something might be, it must pull us bodily, sometimes screaming and kicking, sometimes as if moving into a lover's arms.

How do you understand in general the relationship between everyday life and theatre? Would you concur with Alan Read's argument in Theatre & Everyday Life: An Ethics of Performance *that theatre doesn't fill empty space but, instead, moves into occupied space in order to uncover the relationship between its practices and the everyday?*

Read is quite right. The relationship is a dialectic of pointing not with the index finger but with the thumb: up to identify what we might isolate as our ideal; down to specify what we might see as our less attractive or base dimensions; and wobbling and wiggling to the right and to the left to indicate our politics.

I am reminded of Adrienne Rich's words in What Is Found There: Notebooks on Poetry and Politics:
A poem can't free us from the struggle for existence, but it can uncover desires and appetites buried under the accumulating emergencies of our lives, the fabricated wants and needs we have had urged on us, have accepted as our own. It's not a philosophical or psychological blueprint; it's an instrument for embodied experience. (12–13)
While she is talking about poetry, I think the same would hold for theatre. Would you agree?

Yes. Rich also says in that collection: "We go to poetry because we believe it has something to do with us. We also go to poetry to receive the experience of the *not me*, enter a field of vision we could not otherwise apprehend" (85). This is similar to the space that performers occupy, the space that Richard Schechner describes as "not me, not not me." It is a space that requires the capacity to enter another and to make sense of the encounter.

Are you simply talking about empathy now?

As you know, under the powerful and persuasive hand of Brecht, empathy has become a devil term, a poor substitute for political action. Interviewed by Jill Taft-Kaufman for *Text and Performance Quarterly*, poet Carolyn Forche voiced this same concern. She mentioned that she stopped giving talks about El Salvador because she sensed that people were finding themselves sufficiently noble for simply attending, were making others' tragedies into a commodity. I am sympathetic to those concerns but would maintain that without empathy, it is unlikely that anyone would be motivated to take action on behalf of another. Empathy is a step, an essential one, if people are to move toward one another with understanding and compassion.

That sounds rather Pollyanna. It sounds like old liberal humanism.
The critique of liberal humanism is fairly widespread as well. The critique typically centers on the failure of certain liberal strategies and on narrow conceptions of what constitutes human experience. While these critiques point to important issues that liberal humanists must recognize and act upon, I don't find that they undermine the foundations of liberal humanism. They call instead for expanded strategies for dealing with particular problems, including getting out of the way so that others might occupy the space you were inhabiting, and expanded notions of humankind, breaking from rigid logics that see the world only in terms of a Western, white male, hegemony. This white male sees no reason why liberal humanism cannot accommodate these concerns and, in doing so, offer the best place to stand, a place not without dangers but filled with the potential to make a better world. And yes, that is Pollyanna.

I think you are forgetting a wonderful play you saw several years ago in New York: Stand-Up Tragedy *by Bill Cain. The critics killed it before it had much of a run, but I know you remain extremely fond of it because it demonstrates the inadequacy of liberal ideology. It features a white liberal teacher who empathizes deeply with the plight of one of his Hispanic students, so much so that the teacher can duplicate some of the student's words and actions simultaneously as the student is speaking. The teacher tries to intervene in the student's troubles but only makes matters worse. The play is a forceful critique of the notion that under the flag of liberal humanism, white men might go marching in and save the day.*
Under what other flag would you have white men march?

What is wrong with a flag of revolution or a flag of surrender?
I'm not convinced yet that we must have revolution. Perhaps I will be. But if the revolution were to succeed or if I were to surrender, I would hope that those taking charge would have the hearts of liberal humanists. Perhaps the talk of flags is the problem.

Without flag waving, how do you ground your performance work. All performance, whether implicitly or explicitly, operates under some banner. Is there an escape from the tyranny of flags?
Perhaps not. Perhaps we will never eliminate flags, but we need not wave them in each other's face.

Sometimes there is no other choice.
Perhaps you are right, but I don't much like myself when I decide there is no other choice.

Whether or not you like yourself seems irrelevant to the issue of what might be needed at a given time. I would be quite willing to bury you under the right flag. You are expendable.
Yes, I am. My actions, though, are all I have, all I can control. I side with e. e. cummings when he said in his 1926 introduction to *is 5*, I am "obsessed with Making." And, in the making, I "am abnormally fond of that precision which creates movement." I privilege process over product. What engages me in theatrical practice is the search for the right choice, the exact vocal or bodily gesture that proves telling, that rings true, that competes, as cummings would have it, with roses. That is not to say that the product or final results do not matter; it is, however, to indicate where I think artists need to place their energy.

So you would privilege craft over the thing made and its political consequences?
Craft is the artist's greatest tool. Tools are taken up to reach desired ends. I sense that you are feeling resistant to these ideas, even hostile.

I apologize if I have seemed confrontational, but I didn't anticipate that I would find some of your answers troublesome. Your reliance on poets and the poetic unfolds as an empty rhetoric, at best, a rhetorical trick that seduces for the moment but ultimately says nothing. Furthermore, much of your talk seems dated, anachronistic. Even so, I'm willing to push on. I'll try to be more open, to adopt a more accepting attitude, to live more easily in your reality. Would you discuss your views on directing?
I accept your apology knowing that at any time we can, to borrow a useful cliché, agree to disagree. As to your question: Directing is like holding a sparrow in your hand, squeeze too tightly and it dies, too loosely and it slips away. The sparrow cannot be held for too long, for to do so would be to tame it, would be to ruin its nature. It is held only to ensure its health. After some time, it must be set free, free to fly and land wherever it might, chirping or squawking.

Is the director's job to teach it what to chirp and squawk?
I can accept that as long as one remembers that its egg did not crack open in a cage and that if the environment is not polluted, all birds should be able to sing.

At the risk of letting this metaphor get even further out of hand, would you say that academic theatre provides a comfortable place to nest?

It certainly is fairly comfortable for those who have access to it. Within that community, however, one can think of the level of comfort in a variety of ways. It is comfortable in that it is relatively easy to do theatre, to get stage time, but quite uncomfortable if the measure of success is the distance from Broadway or a professional career. Too often our students hold only such standards for determining the worth of their training. Comfort can also be a way of thinking about what constitutes a conducive working space. Too little comfort and it is difficult to feel safe enough to create. Too much comfort and it is difficult to feel vulnerable enough to create.

Vulnerable?

Yes, stemming from the Latin "vulnerare," to wound. Art, I think, often speaks from our wounds.

Is it the performer's task, then, to seek experiences that wound?

The performer need not *seek* such experiences; life will supply quite enough. And what life doesn't inflict, imagination can provide.

Anna Deavere Smith asked in Performing Arts Journal *(May/September 1995): "Is it possible . . . we have spent too much time training our students to mirror ourselves, to show the world what's inside of the artist rather than the world around the artist?" How do you respond to Smith's rhetorical question? Or, to ask the question more pointedly, aren't you privileging the "inside" when you talk of speaking from wounds?*

Your concern seems to be that the notion of wounds, of speaking from the inside, seems to return us to the Romantic era, to Wordsworth's "spontaneous overflow of powerful feelings recollected in tranquility." You worry that the political will drop out as one loses oneself in a "host of golden daffodils," that the world will not be "too much with us." I am not unsympathetic to that concern. I too find that the self can become self-absorbed, self-indulgent. We see this often when performers work with personal narratives. Wounds, though, are the source, not the cause, of artistic utterance. Often, what is *inside* the artist is what the artist finds *around* himself/herself. I think Smith's work is proof that what is inside can be worth getting outside not only for purely artistic reasons but also for political ones.

Since you mentioned personal narratives, perhaps we can spend some time discussing that growing performance phenomenon. I know that you have taught courses centering on personal narratives, that you have directed shows that were based in them, and that you are completing a book project that uses them quite liberally. Would you specify the characteristics of a good personal narrative?

The personal narratives to which I find myself most attracted have two primary features: (1) the story told points beyond the self; and (2) the story told reminds you that consequences happen on an individual level. In other words, politics only matter as they unravel in individual lives, and individual lives only matter when they can make a political difference. Otherwise, performances of personal narratives become either solipsistic dribble or hollow sloganizing. I try to work in the space between those two extremes.

How do you explain the attraction to personal narratives in the age of the fragmented self?

I had a dream not too long ago that bubbles, with my name written on them, were floating around the room where I was sleeping. Each bubble contained some aspect of me. I couldn't get out of bed until I gathered all the bubbles. Personal narratives are a way of gathering the bubbles.

Can they be gathered? Is there such a thing as a unified self? Perhaps the difficulty is that we are fragmented, often operating from multiple positions.

I never lose sight of my other me's. When the need arises, I simply place them to the side. I try to accommodate my fragmented selves within my pluralist one. I exchange my instability for agency.

I will resist saying that you simply do not understand, that you have not mined as fully as you might contemporary literature on the crisis of representation. Instead, in the spirit of a cooperative gesture, I'll ask you about pluralism, a position most scholars greet with considerable skepticism. How do you answer the charge that the pluralist is actually a relativist who doesn't have the guts to stand up for his/her beliefs?

As a pluralist, I take a stand each time I adopt a different critical stance, including the burden of arguing that the stance I've adopted at that point in time is worth adopting and including the burden of recognizing the nature of the knowledge a given position might generate. That is far from saying any position will do and far from ducking ideological commitments. For me, the crisis in representation occurs when one falls into a deconstructive abyss. It is difficult to take a stand when swirling downward. All one hears is this faint echo coming to the surface: "Nothing is stable, nothing is stable."

I take it you are suspicious of such claims!

Deconstruction without reconstruction is little more than a game of wit. Despite the great charm and sophistication of the game, it often leaves one unsatisfied. I've written a little parody of the position. Should I share it?

I guess. I've indulged you this far.

As you know, I'm always a little hesitant to share any of my poems, but here it is:

Deconstructive Rag

Difference is in

Defer
Don't refer

Supplement
Don't compliment

Transform
Don't conform

Difference is in

Trace this place
Into grace

Don't reflect
Just genuflect

Language is hot
People are not

What I wrote
Take note

Is here
There, everywhere

Present absent
Loaded toaded

Difference is in.

I won't bother reminding you that you often refer to yourself as a fifth-rate poet and that writing a parody of a position you often employ is hardly in the pluralist spirit. Perhaps, though, we might end by asking you, setting aside the question of quality, what it means to you to be a practicing poet, performer, and director?

It is to feel vain and vulnerable simultaneously. Vain in that it requires an arrogance of the highest degree to believe that others might want to consume what you have to offer. Stephen Dobyns's little poem, "Vanity," includes the lines: "I write this, / you read this." Vulnerable in that it demands a giving of one's self, a self that may be dismissed or destroyed. From his poem "Contingencies," I quote Dobyns again: "I become / a glass target among all things pointed and haphazard." It is to feel as if one were china in a china shop, watching the bull enter.

I sense that you are glad the interview is over?

Well, your responses do become tiresome, predictable. It is difficult for me to listen to the same old platitudes, cliché after cliché. You started our talk by noting that performers assume different relationships to words, but implicit in your argument and in your ideas throughout this interview is the privileging of an ideal relationship to your words. In short, for you, there is a correct stance. Your pluralism is nothing more than another dogma authorizing the same practices that silence those who do not fit into your schemes. You try to accommodate the political injustices you see with lip service, minor tinkerings here and there, but nothing really changes. The oppressive structures stay in place, insisting that performers and audiences come to performance with certain assumptions in place. Just consider who remains the master in your logic, who is the godlike narrator empowered to tell all, who must produce and consume by your standards.

Would you have us abandon standards?

I would have you recognize what standards are an arbitrary set of values, culturally and historically based, that sanctions some forms of discourse while shutting down others. Your standards colonize. You measure all others by your own terms. You view all others from your own preferred positions. You only deem acceptable what fits under your own preestablished norms.

What would you have instead?

Places of negotiation. Places where no answers are set or predetermined. Places of encounter. Places where all are positioned together, possessing equal status, hands forward, turning and twisting around one another, each finger formulating a different course of action.

What keeps the hands from turning into fists?

What I'm talking about is work that tries to make a difference. At times,

one might get punched. That is a small price to pay for genuine change. Existing in the space I am describing is not an easy space to occupy, but I believe that our future depends upon our ability to do so.
Aren't you being a bit melodramatic?

Only from where you exist.
Perhaps. Perhaps a useful way to end our little encounter is to quote some lines from another Stephen Dobyns poem, "The Way It Goes or the Proper Use of Leisure Time":

> Now all my words are bricks
> and I have built myself a small penitentiary.
> . . . .
> With intense effort, I turn the bricks
> back into words. They flutter and fall
> like dying bats. Here is one called
> Help, and another, Haste.

Ronald J. Pelias teaches performance studies at Southern Illinois University at Carbondale. He is the author of *Performance Studies: The Interpretation of Aesthetic Texts*. His research has been published in such journals as *Text and Performance Quarterly*, *Theatre Research International*, *Quarterly Journal of Speech*, and *Journal of Dramatic Theory and Criticism*. His poems have appeared most recently in *Negative Capability*, *Parnassus Literary Journal*, *The Small Pond*, and *Palo Alto Review*.

Benedictine University Library
Mesa Campus
225 E. Main Street
Mesa, AZ 85201

gradschl@siu.edu